DECEIVED

By: Keisha Mayo

Publishing

Autograph Page

Autograph this book to someone who needs help being set free from deception.

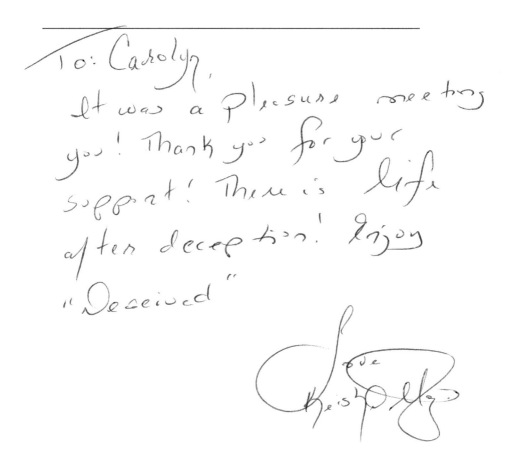

To: Carolyn,
It was a pleasure meeting you! Thank you for your support! There is life after deception! Enjoy "Deceived"

Love
Kristodello

Acknowledgments

Grandma - To the late Evangelist Susie G. Goldson; thank you for your unconditional love, prayers, concerns, support and encouragement. Thank you for interceding on my behalf when I could not do it for myself. Love always, Your Jelly Bean.

Daddy - To the late Carl E. Mayo, Sr.; thank you for always being there for me.
I love and miss you so much.

Uncle Steve - To the late Steven Williams, Sr.; thank you for watching over your niece and making sure she did not get charged for something she did not do.
I love you and miss you.

Mom - Words cannot express how much I love you. Thank you for your unconditional love. You were there for me when others turned their backs. If there were a million mothers in a barrel and I had to pick one, I would pick you every time.

Lisa Mayo, Carl E. Mayo, Jr., Lynn Mayo, - I love you all from the bottom of my heart. You all have played a part in my growth during this tough time.

Latarsha Bullock - Words cannot express how much I appreciate you! I thank God for placing you in my family. God has so much in store for you. I love you sis!

First Lady Tracy Hopkins - Thank you for your love and encouraging words. I could always count on you to lift my spirit when I was down.
I love you Big Sis!

Linzette Smith - Thank you for always being an ear. No matter how late I called, you would be there to encourage me. I love you sis and there is nothing you can do about it.

Takeytha Johnson - Thank you for being an ear and constantly reminding me that brighter days are ahead. I love you!

Iva Cunningham - Thank you for our talks, your love and your prayers. I could always count on you to lift my spirits. You have helped me tremendously with finishing this book. I am grateful for the time you took out of your busy schedule to put a smile on my face. You said to me "I am going to help you because I want you to be happy", that touched my heart to know that you love me that much. Auntie, I love you from the bottom of my heart!

Miriam Williams - We have been best friends since Elementary School and I thank God for placing you in my life. You have always had my back and made sure I was always protected. I love you sis! Tyson has nothing on you.

Reverend Patricia Reeves - Thank you for everything you have done for me. You have given me so much of your time, advice and knowledge on the process of writing this book. I thank God for you! Love you Pat.

Sandra Flowers-Jones - I thank God for placing me in your life. You were there for the tears, hurt and pain. We may have different mothers but you are definitely my big sister. You are always concerned about my well-being and for that, I love you!

<u>Pastor Robert Goldson</u> - Thank you for stepping in the place of my dad when he went home to be with the Lord. You have done a wonderful job so far and I love you from the bottom of my heart.

<u>First Lady June Goldson</u> - Thank you for your timeless efforts in helping review the book. Your love and patience is greatly appreciated. I love you!

<u>Grace Francis</u> - Thank you for constantly encouraging me to complete the book! I know you have been waiting a long time. I love you!

<u>Tarsha Swindell</u> – Thank you for your love, prayers and concern. Thank you for praying for me when I could not pray for myself. Thank you for allowing God to use you to encourage me. I love you Big Sis!

Table of Contents

Introduction

This book is designed to encourage individuals that no matter what you go through in life, you can make it with Jesus Christ on your side. The bible says, *"And let us not be weary in well doing: for in due season we shall reap if we faint not."* *Galatians 6:9.* My prayer is that this story reaches everyone who may be going through similar situations and feel they can't talk about it! "And the Lord said, *''Simon, Simon, behold, Satan hath desired to have you, that he may sift you as wheat."* *Luke 22:31.*

The devil's desire is to isolate you, tear you down and make you afraid or embarrassed to speak out. So you find yourself dealing with it all alone while the enemy is tormenting your mind. But God reminds us in *1 Corinthians 10:13,* *"There hath no temptation taken you but such as is common to man: but God is faithful, who will not suffer you to be tempted above that ye are able; but will with the temptation also make a way to escape, that ye may bear it."*

Thank God for a way to escape! The enemy will also try and deceive you and make you feel that you have it all together. Life will take you on a roller coaster ride. Just when you think the ride is over, it keeps on going. No longer will you be tormented, isolated, deceived, bitter, angry, and frustrated by what life throws your way.

Chapter 1

A Knight In Shining Armor

Hi. My name is Sabrina and my best friend's name is Nicole. Nicole has a story to tell but I may have to be the one who tells it. Have you ever had a friend who is so shy and quiet that when the Mr. Softie Man asks "what kind of ice cream do you want?" that she whispers, "toasted almond" in your ear so you can tell him? That's me and Nicole. She is the whisperer. I am the spokesperson. We're not girls on the playground anymore but sometimes, even now, she whispers in my ear. I have the feeling, though, that before Nicole's story is over --- she'll be speaking up for herself.

Her story is a tale of deception. Deception. I've been thinking a lot about that word. What it means and how it feels to be deceived; tricked; deluded. Maybe you're thinking that you could never be deceived. I know that's what I always thought – I'm way too street wise to be deceived. But then I heard Nicole's story.

This story begins with a young girl named Nicole Watts who was born and raised in the South Bronx. Nicole overcame so many obstacles although she grew up in one of the roughest housing projects in the Bronx. She vowed that although she lived in the projects, she would not become a product of where she lived. Nicole's grandmother, Susie Lawson, and mother, Beverly Watts, are Evangelists. Evangelist meaning they would go out and preach in public. That meant everyone was in church on Sundays. The good thing about it was that Nicole's mother, Evangelist Watts, allowed her kids to be kids. She allowed her children to go to parties and have fun but they knew they were going to be in church every Sunday. Nicole was very shy growing up and she was also the youngest out of four siblings. Nevertheless, she was very attractive, fashionable and always dreamed of the finer things in life.

Nicole would always sit in church with her coat on until the end of service. Nicole's grandmother would always ask her mother "What is wrong with that child? Why is she always sitting in the church with her coat on?" Nicole's problem was that she just did not want to be there. She always felt her family was the sore thumb because everyone at Second Chance Pentecostal Church was related. *"Train up a child in the way he should go; and when he is old, he will not depart from it". Proverbs 22:6*

Nicole recalls a short, brown skinned, four eyed boy named Ramon Williams, Jr. who was the second to youngest child in the Williams' household. Both of their families attended Second Chance. Ramon appeared to be a quiet person who kept to himself. Nicole does remember Ramon interacting with one guy named Willie. Willie was a member of Grace Temple Pentecostal Church. Whenever the two churches fellowshipped, they would always hang out together. Ramon's father, Ramon Williams, Sr., was an Elder at Second Chance Pentecostal Church. Ramon's parents were really strict and it appeared he had no life. His life was built around the church. He was in church on Sundays and weekdays. One Sunday Ramon was talking to Nicole's brother while service was going on and Elder Williams gave Ramon Jr. the meanest look. You could see in Ramon's face how scared he was. He later told Nicole that he got a beating that night.

Ramon was known for his singing ability at Second Chance. He was always called to lead a song or sing a solo and everyone at the church loved to hear Ramon sing. They would always talk about Ramon or a young girl named Cindy. Ramon was going to be a lawyer when he grew up and Cindy was going to be a doctor. I believe Ramon felt he had to live up to other's dreams and aspirations. People have to live life according to their dreams and not what others want for them. God's will for our lives is what matters the most. *"For I know the thoughts that I think toward you, saith the Lord, thoughts of peace, and not of evil, to give you an expected end".* *Jeremiah 29:11*

Nicole eventually found out that Ramon had a crush on her. Ramon told Nicole that his cousin Sonia said to him,

"You would never get Nicole because you can't afford her". Although Nicole knew Ramon liked her, she was not interested at all. Ramon was always afraid to speak to Nicole. Mrs. Watts caught Ramon staring at Nicole in church with a little mirror. He would use the mirror to watch Nicole if she was sitting a few rows behind him. Nicole never noticed because she was not paying him any attention. Ramon would always put his cousin Sonia up to his dirty work.

During one service, Sonia handed Nicole a piece of paper and said it was from Ramon. When Nicole opened it, it was a picture that Ramon drew for her with her name on it. Nicole handed the paper back to Sonia and stated, "He spelled my name wrong". The next time he saw Nicole at church, he drew another picture and this time her name was spelled correctly. Nicole still did not accept the picture because she did not like Ramon and did not want to lead him on. His feelings were hurt but she just could not have him believe something would become of the two. Sonia told Nicole that Ramon used to bug her about hooking them up together.

Sonia told Nicole that it got to the point where she was going to tell Nicole because he was too scared to tell her himself. One night Sonia called Nicole and told her that Ramon liked her and wanted to take her to the movies. When Ramon found out what she had done, he was very angry and felt as though his cousin betrayed him. Ramon had a fear of rejection and didn't want to take a chance of getting hurt again. Nicole expressed to Sonia that she did not want to go out with Ramon because she was not into him. She ended up hurting his feelings anyway.

When Nicole turned 18, she left Second Chance Pentecostal Church and began visiting other churches. Although Nicole did not want to be a member at Second Chance, she never wanted to leave the church completely. After months of visiting different churches, Nicole felt that God led her to join Fire Baptized Holiness Church. Nicole would visit Second Chance every now and then for their yearly Friends and Family Day services or when her mother had to preach. Whenever Nicole came to visit, she would attend with her boyfriend Karl. She found out later that Ramon would get mad when he saw the two of them together.

After a few years had passed, Nicole visited Second Chance for a special service. This was the first time that Nicole and Ramon finally had a conversation after years of a simple hello and goodbye. Nicole and Karl were broken up by this time. They did not talk about anything important but Ramon asked her what church she was attending. They exchanged telephone numbers and told each other to keep in touch. Ramon called Nicole two days later. Their conversations were very quick in the beginning because they didn't know what to say to each other.

Ramon would always act like he did not understand what she was saying. For instance, if Nicole was giving him a number to write down, Ramon would always mix the numbers up. Ramon did not realize it, but Nicole was getting very annoyed. He later told Nicole that he was doing it on purpose. The next time they spoke, Ramon asked her if she was going to Second Chance's Sunday School Convention. Of all the years Nicole's family attended Second Chance, she hardly wanted to be there let alone go to a convention. Nicole told him that she would get back to him and let him know if she was going to go or not. By the time they had their next conversation; Nicole told him that she decided to go.

Nicole's best friend Denise decided to go with them. Friends, Tommy and Willie also decided to ride in the car with Ramon and Nicole. They made arrangements to leave New York City for North Carolina at eleven o'clock PM. Eleven o'clock came and went and there was no sign of Ramon or the car.

Nicole and Denise started to get very impatient. Nicole believed in being punctual and valued time. She did not like for someone to give a time and not stand by it. Willie and Ramon were getting frustrated because Nicole kept calling and Denise and Nicole were getting frustrated because they were getting tired of waiting. They finally told them that they were having problems with the van. They eventually called back around one in the morning letting them know that they were going to take Willie's father's van.

Finally, they were on their way to Greenville, North Carolina. Tommy told the group, "If I start to scratch my head that means I am tired". After a few hours of driving,

Tommy began to scratch his head. Nicole saw him scratching his head but was so tired that she only remembered what he said after they ended up in the ditch. *"For thou, Lord, wilt bless the righteous; with favor wilt thou compass him as with a shield" Psalms 5:12.*

Although the experience was scary, Ramon made Nicole feel very comfortable. Everyone sat on the side of the road until they recuperated. The journey began again and it was Ramon's time to drive. Nicole sat on the passenger side talking with him to keep him awake. God gave them traveling mercies and they made it there safe. *"Be not afraid of sudden fear, neither of the desolation of the wicked, when it cometh. For the Lord shall be thy confidence, and shall keep thy foot from being taken". Proverbs 3:25-26*

They were having a great time at the convention. Nicole met some of Ramon's family members that lived down there. Ramon's cousin Rocky asked him "Oh, is that your girl?" Ramon replied "I want it to be". Nicole got a big kick out of that. Nicole did not have to spend her money for anything while down there. Ramon would always tell her to put her money away. When they came back to New York, Nicole and Ramon spoke on the phone every night. They were now officially boyfriend and girlfriend!

Nicole would always tease him about being a church boy. Ramon always acted as if he had never heard a secular song before. Nicole would go to Ramon's house on holidays or if her friend drove her. Ramon would normally take a two hour ride to Nicole's house. He said he did not have a problem taking the trains. It would be hailing, sleeting or snowing outside and Ramon would press his way to come see her. Mind you, he had a two hour ride going and coming. Nicole was in heaven. She felt as though she had finally found her true love.

Chapter 2

Will the Real Ramon Please Stand Up

R amon was always there when Nicole needed him. He always had an encouraging word to offer when she was down. Nicole can honestly say that Ramon never made her pay for anything. Ramon eventually left Second Chance Pentecostal Church and joined Fire Baptized Holiness Church with Nicole. Nicole was a member of the choir and Ramon joined the choir shortly after he joined the church. Ramon would praise God Sunday after Sunday, whether it was shouting or walking around the church giving God praise.

Everyone seemed to love Ramon. Ramon could do no wrong. Their church family loved Ramon as well. Some people in the church would call him Ramon the lawyer. Ramon was not the same little boy Nicole knew at Second Chance Pentecostal Church. He was still pretty quiet but was beginning to come out of his shell. He was funny, loving, respectful, well mannered, educated and giving. Nicole's family thought the world of Ramon.

Ramon told Nicole that he was attending Gateway University for his undergraduate studies. Gateway University is a neighboring Ivy League school which is very selective with their admission process and vigorous programs. At the time, Nicole was attending school nearby at Bright Waters College. He always shared with Nicole how hard it was to enroll in that school. He told her that he got accepted because of his grades. He also received scholarships which aided him with tuition. He told Nicole that he and his dad had to meet before the admissions committee before being accepted into Gateway.

Ramon told Nicole that when they interviewed the Caucasian kids, he would see them coming out the interview boasting and bragging about how easy and quick the interview was, unlike Ramon's interview, which was long and intense. Ramon would go to school, go to work, and meet Nicole at her school. After he picked her up from school, he would make sure she got home safely.

Nicole never understood how he always did so much in one day. He would tell her that his class was cancelled or they let them out early. Nicole would ask Ramon, "When do you find time to study?" He would tell her that he studied either on the train going home or on his way to his job at the bookstore. There would be days when Nicole would stay up late studying and Ramon would be there helping her. No matter what time he got home the night before, Ramon would still go to school, work and meet up with Nicole. Nicole would constantly ask Ramon about his grades. She said that she wanted to see them. Nicole didn't notice before but Ramon had an excuse for everything. He told her that his professors did not finish processing the grades. He told her that he knew his grades even though he did not receive them on paper. He told her that he had two A's, one A- and one B+.

Nicole and Ramon ran into a guy on the street that Ramon knew. When the guy walked away, Ramon told Nicole that he was in one of his classes he taught at Summerville College. Nicole thought to herself, this guy is really intelligent. Ramon was young, a student at one of the top schools, on scholarship, has good grades and taught at Summerville College. Ramon told Nicole that he was meeting with the school dean to protest the B+ he received. He claimed the professor was prejudiced. He told her that it was not the first time he had to go before the school's administration to get his grade changed.

One thing Nicole can honestly say is that Ramon motivated her to do well in school. Before she started dating Ramon, she would get B's, B+s and A's here and there. Now Nicole was getting straight A's. Nicole felt really good about herself. *"Study to shew thyself approved unto God, a workman that needeth not to be ashamed, rightly dividing the word of truth". II Timothy 2:15*

Ramon told Nicole that he enrolled in the five year MBA program at Gateway College. Nicole could not get over Ramon and his endeavors. He had it going on in her eyes. Nicole just couldn't understand how he would always be at her house and still found time to study. He told Nicole that

Gateway was very expensive and he paid off two $15,000 loans. Nicole asked him how he was able to pay off the loans and he explained that he worked a lot of overtime. He said that he had a good job with the Post Office which Nicole realized later that it was not listed on his resume. Well Nicole felt she had her own thing going on so she didn't have time to run behind someone to see if they were lying.

Every time he would see his school advertised on television, he would get so excited. He told everyone about being a part of the Honor Society. He said that he was on the Dean's list nine consecutive semesters. Ramon was also a member of a nationally recognized prominent African-American male fraternity. He also worked with a program called the Upward Bounds Community Outreach program. This program was geared towards youth and helping them excel in life.

Ramon told everyone that he was graduating Summa Cum Laude. Nicole recalls a time Ramon's brother Carlton called him to ask about enrolling in Gateway University and Ramon told him "You will never get accepted to that school because you don't have good grades". He said that Carlton was the only one in the family that did not do well in school. He even told Nicole that the Honor Society gave him a loan to pay for one of his semesters.

Nicole was so proud of Ramon that she told him she was going to throw him a party. Ramon told her, "No, I don't want a party because I don't feel like I have accomplished anything". Nicole didn't understand how he could feel that way given all the remarkable things he was involved in but decided that perhaps he was more insecure than she had realized. He told her to wait until he graduated from law school to throw him a party.

Ramon left Nicole's parents' house around 1 a.m. one morning and he called when he arrived home. Ramon sounded shaken up when he called. Nicole asked him what happened and he stated that the cab he was riding in was stopped by the cops. He said the cops pulled him out of the car because he fit the description of a man they were looking for. He said that he proceeded to tell the cops that he knows his rights. The cop then stated to him, "Oh you are one of those stupid law school kids who think they know everything". He said they let him go after that. The next day, Ramon told Nicole that he shared the situation with one of his law professors who in turn made a phone call which led to the two cops getting fired. Nicole asked Ramon if he was scared the cops would come after him and he said "No, I am not scared".

One evening, Ramon and Nicole went to Willow A.M.E. Church in Queens, N.Y. The speaker was Reverend Todd Wilson. He began to prophesy to different people within the congregation. This man was very powerful. There was a child screaming and crying in the back of the church. Reverend Wilson walked over to the child, did something with his hands and the baby calmed down. In the middle of service, he told the child's mother, "Don't worry, he will speak again." They did not hear from the baby until the service was over. The next thing Nicole knew, he was calling Ramon out. Ramon walked over to him and he began to prophesy about how Ramon was going to have a problem paying for school. Ramon told Nicole that he whispered in his ear the exact amount that he would owe the school. Nicole did not know if Ramon told the preacher what he was going to school for but he said that Ramon was going to open a law firm on Wall Street. After he finished giving Ramon his word, he told Ramon to begin to praise God. Ramon started praising God and crying.

At that time, Ramon was working at Read and Relax Bookstore. Nicole did not know how much money Ramon brought home but he seemed to be very responsible. They bought so many gifts for each other. Nicole felt like they had so much in common.

One night Ramon and Nicole were hanging out at the Sho-Town Café in Times Square with their friends Sharon and Jerry. Nicole got the surprise of her life. Ramon surprised Nicole with a gorgeous engagement ring, flowers and a cake that read "Will you marry me?" Everyone sitting in their section was screaming and cheering. Even people that did not know them cheered for the newly engaged couple. The Sho-Town Café has since closed but Nicole would never forget that memorable moment.

Ramon was now in law school at Shoreway University. Nicole never saw the MBA degree he received at Gateway University but like so many times before, she overlooked many signs that things did not quite fit together. That's what happens in the midst of deception. Sometimes we are deceived by someone and sometimes, *we deceive ourselves.* Nicole asked Ramon where his degree was and he told her that he could not get it until he paid off his school loan. When she asked about the graduation, he told her that the school made a mistake and scheduled another graduation on the same day. He told her that the date was changed. Two weeks later, Nicole asked him about the ceremony and he stated "The school decided to cancel the ceremony". Nicole did not bother bringing it up again.

Chapter 3

All that Glitters is not Gold

The big day finally arrived! Ramon and Nicole were getting married. They had a big beautiful wedding with about 250 guests in attendance. Nicole was such a beautiful bride and Ramon looked pretty sharp himself. It was a beautiful sun filled day; the perfect day for the perfect wedding! They got married at their home church, Fire Baptized Holiness Church. Nicole had to admit that everything turned out wonderfully and ran smoothly. The reception was at a beautiful catering hall called the West End Manor.

The couple spent a lot of money for their wedding. The videographer told them that it was one of the best weddings he had ever done. Ramon wrote a beautiful song which he sang to Nicole at the reception. Everyone danced, talked, ate and had a wonderful time. Nicole could not believe she was finally married. After the reception, they had an after party at Nicole's sister Ann's house. It was such a perfect and beautiful day for the love birds. They stayed up all night until it was time to board the plane for their honeymoon. Nicole was petrified of planes so she wanted to sleep once she got on the plane. Sadly, while on the plane, she was wired so she couldn't even sleep. Ramon and Nicole were honeymooning in St. Croix, Virgin Islands. They did not have a direct flight so they had a layover in Puerto Rico. When they got to Puerto Rico, they had to board a plane that seated 20 people.

Nicole was scared to death! They felt every air pocket and heard every loud noise. Nicole began to panic and started crying. Ramon hugged her, told her not to worry, and that turbulence happens all the time. After they departed the plane, Ramon said that he was scared as well but was trying to be strong for her. They both had a good laugh after that. Nicole's voice got so low I could barely hear her as she continued her story. "My perfect wedding day ended that evening," her voice trembled. "I was a virgin and had vowed to save herself for her husband. And as far as I knew, Ramon was a virgin as well. So I knew that things would be awkward and that we would both be very nervous. But I was not expecting what happened that night at all!"

As it turns out, Ramon could not get an erection to save his life. Nicole could not believe what was happening. After all these years, here she saved herself for the man of her dreams and for what? How could this be happening to someone like Nicole? After several useless attempts all she could do was turn over in the bed and cry.

Ramon began to cry hysterically saying "My mother knew there was something wrong with my body and she never told me". In the midst of Nicole crying she thought, "you are a grown man, why would your mother know what's wrong with your body?" The next day they decided to go to the beach and do other fun things to forget about what just happened. They realized that they could not forget for long because they had to go back to the room. They tried to become one again with no successful results. Nicole just cried and cried. She could not believe that it was her honeymoon and her husband could not make love to her.

The rest of the week consisted of having fun during the day and being miserable at night. They went to many shows, went swimming, sightseeing and Ramon even won the limbo contest! They laughed and socialized with many of the other guests at the resort and celebrated --- just like any other newly married couple. But, inevitably they had to return to their honeymoon suite filled with dread and sadness. Each night ended with one failed attempt after the other. On their way back home, Ramon and Nicole kept up a constant stream of chatter and laughter talking about all the fun activities of the week. No one spoke about the fact that the intimacy that everyone anticipates on a honeymoon had never occurred......Deception.

When Ramon and Nicole returned from their honeymoon, they moved into their new apartment. Without even discussing it, they both put on the façade of "the happy newlyweds". Sometimes we participate in a deception because the truth is too painful to face or we just don't know how to break through the wall of silence and talk about the reality. So they did what we all do when we don't want to expose our pain; they pretended. Nicole looked at me with her eyes filled with tears, "I felt lost and so alone. This was a secret I had to keep. I was sad, frustrated and confused."

In spite of that, Nicole stated that God had really blessed them financially and that in *that* way, they seemed to be on the same page. The apartment was fully furnished the first week they returned home. They had paid for the entire wedding and did not owe anyone anything. That was great and something that lots of people can't say.

But, weeks had passed and the marriage still was not consummated. Ramon was still working at the bookstore but he transferred to a location closer to home. They planned their housewarming two months after they moved in. Plans had to change because Ramon's mother passed away a week before the housewarming. Nicole had to call everyone to cancel.

When Nicole arrived at the hospital, Ramon was standing over his mom. As Nicole moved closer to Ramon, she heard him crying saying "Mom, I am going to do the right thing. I am going to be a man, ma". He kept repeating it over and over. Nicole stood there wondering what he meant by that because in her eyes he *was* a man. Nicole said, "At that moment, I began to consider that I didn't know all that I needed to know about my husband." Nicole honestly believed his mother knew something about her son. She may not have known everything about her son but she knew something.

Nicole recalls visiting Ramon's parent's home and his mother tried to tell Nicole something. She started off by saying "If you both work, you make him…. ". Ramon immediately ran over to her and childishly covered her mouth. He started over talking her with nonsensical noises. Nicole would never know what she was trying to tell her.

The family had two funeral services. One service was at Second Chance Pentecostal Church and the other was down south in her hometown. At this point, Ramon seemed to be taking his mother's death very well. Nicole had to tell him that it was okay to cry. Nicole made him feel confident in knowing that if he needed someone to talk to she was there for him.

Ramon always told Nicole that his mother was the only person he could talk to. He would tell her that he did not have a relationship with his dad. In Nicole's eyes, he hated his dad. He would say that his dad was only there for him financially. He said that his dad never spent time with him or took him to a baseball game. He felt that his dad's main priority was his twin sisters. He hated one sister and loved the other. He refused to let his sister be a part of their big day. Ramon's twin sisters were much older than he. Even when the two got married, if it were not for Nicole, his family would not have heard from Ramon. He would always tell Nicole that he did not want to be like his father. He would say that his mother was his only outlet.

He would admire Nicole and her relationship with her mother and grandmother. He felt Nicole had two people she could talk to about anything. With Ramon still dealing with the death of his mom, Nicole still did not pressure Ramon about the sex issue. At that point, Nicole could not talk to anyone, not even her mother or grandmother because she was too embarrassed. How do you get married, live with a man for months and never consummate the marriage? She thought that she would have to take that to her grave. By this time, Nicole considered them married roommates with no benefits. She felt isolated and alone with her secret as her only companion.

A few months later, Nicole and Ramon received a call from his dad, Elder Williams. He stated that he received a credit card bill that did not belong to him. He thought Ramon used his social security number for a credit card. Ramon denied it and said that the company made a mistake. Ramon said that he took out a school loan and he had to give his father's information. He said that they probably mixed up the social security numbers.

A few days later, Elder Williams and Ramon's brother Carlton visited Nicole and Ramon's house. Elder Williams had made a couple of phone calls to the credit card companies. Ramon's dad even went as far as trying to pay off one of the credit cards to clear his name. He asked Nicole to type up a letter for him to send to the credit card company stating that he was not the credit card holder. Ramon said that he would take the letter to be notarized the next day and send it off. Nicole also typed up a budget for Ramon so he could pay his father back. Ramon never paid off the other credit card bills. He was supposed to use the money he received from his mom to pay them off.

Ramon was still a student at Shoreway University. Even with everything going on, Nicole had yet to see Ramon studying. Nicole said to him "OK, we live together now, why do I never see you studying?" His excuse was that he liked to study when she was asleep. Nicole then asked him if he was really in school. Ramon replied "Yes, I am in school". At that time, God was trying to reveal something to Nicole but she still could not put her finger on it. Now that Nicole asked Ramon about school, she would wake up to an open law book on the living room table as if he was reading it the night before.

Nicole was really disciplined about saving money and would keep a box in the house with a few dollars to use in case of emergencies. She started to notice twenty dollars or sometimes forty dollars was missing. Although she didn't want to admit it to herself, she realized that the problems with Ramon and his character kept growing. She learned her lesson and put all her money in the bank. At first she thought she was messing up her balance. Nicole confronted him about the missing money and started yelling at Ramon to the point where her mother had to come over and intercede.

At this point, Nicole's mom realized there were problems in the marriage, but Nicole still did not have the nerve to tell her that Ramon could not have sex. Ramon explained his petty thievery by saying that Shoreway was harassing him for payments for the loan. He claimed that they told him that if he didn't come up with the money, he was not going to graduate. Nicole finally put him on a payment plan to pay back the money that he took out the house. He would not have to pay her back if he just asked for the money. Ramon stole from Nicole once again but this time he thought he would return the money before she noticed. Nicole went off on him once again.

Ramon started having problems at the bookstore. He claimed his boss was prejudiced. It seems like everyone was prejudiced in his eyes. He told Nicole that he resigned but by this time, she didn't trust much of what he told her and figured that he had probably been fired. Nicole found a five page evaluation in his drawer which stated that he did not meet the requirements to be an Assistant Manager. Ramon asked her to update his resume and between the two of them they produced a resume the top 500 companies would have wanted to hire him.

Chapter 4

In Sickness & In Health...
But It Was a Show

Ramon and Nicole's first year anniversary was coming up and they could not go away because Ramon just started his job at Hillside Bank. They ended up going to a Marriott Hotel in Jersey where they had a good time. Again, they tried to do things that were fun. This was Nicole's first wedding anniversary and she still did not have an intimate relationship with her husband. Nicole did not believe anyone picked up on her unhappiness.

However, she knew just how miserable she was. Enough is enough, Nicole thought. Her frustration had reached its limit. She told him that when they returned home, he must go to the doctor and find out a possible solution to the problem. He took a long time to go to the doctor because he was afraid of what they were going to tell him.

Ramon finally made his appointment to see the medical specialist. Nicole accompanied Ramon to the doctor. The urologist said that one of his testicles was under developed and his penis was heightened. However, this did not explain why he could not have sexual intercourse. The doctor suggested that Ramon take home a machine and attach it to his penis at night to monitor his erections. Ramon did not have any money so Nicole charged the cost of the machine to her credit card. Nicole was tired of living a lie and needed to get to the bottom of what was happening.

Nicole recalls one day they were walking down the street and she started a conversation about the lack of intimacy in their relationship. Out of nowhere, Ramon started acting like he was having an asthma attack. Ramon only got sick when a topic was brought up that he did not want to discuss. That day, they ended up in the emergency room –

that's how desperate he was to maintain the façade.... The Deception.

Ramon was now graduating from law school and everyone was so proud. And in spite of their lack of intimacy, Nicole was the most proud of his accomplishment. She looked at me with tears shining brightly "I always thought that once the stress was off of him, maybe then we would have a real marriage." One Sunday at church, Bishop White had the congregation give him a standing ovation because of his accomplishment. The church was filled with screams and cheers. Ramon stood up proudly with a big smile on his face while the entire congregation cheered. Ramon even helped one of the ladies from their church win a case against her husband. It was all she wrote after that. To Nicole it seemed as though everyone wanted advice after that.

One Sunday Bishop White called Ramon in the office. When Ramon came upstairs, Nicole asked him what he wanted and Ramon replied "he needed some legal information". While Bishop White was preaching he started explaining a legal term. Bishop White asked Ramon in front of the congregation "Did I explain that correctly?" Ramon replied "Yes, you did." Nicole had to give it to Ramon because he was very knowledgeable when it came to the law.

Ramon and Nicole had a meeting with Bishop White. Ramon told him that his desire was to work with the youth department. He told Bishop White a little about his background and how he worked with the Upward Bounds program. Bishop told Ramon that once he gets the youth department off the ground he would let him know. Nicole asked if she could help as well. He told her that it would be good for the youth department to see a young couple working together in the ministry.

Ramon and Nicole were now youth leaders. They worked as a team along with the other four youth leaders. They were really starting to get involved in the church. Sister Tammy was a school teacher and she told Ramon that she was having career day at her school and wanted him to be one of the speakers. The next time they saw Sister Tammy, she said that the kids at the school really enjoyed him and wanted him to come back. One of Nicole's co-workers was going through a situation with her son. He could have been arrested. Ramon spoke to her on the phone for a long time giving her legal advice. She thanked Nicole over and over again for Ramon helping her. The case was eventually dropped. Law school, ministry leadership, lots of compliments and encouragement.....all of these wonderful things were happening for Ramon. Nicole held tight to the hope that one day soon their joy would be complete.

Nicole called Ramon's job one day and a female co-worker picked up the phone. She asked Nicole how she was doing. Ramon always said he wanted us to hang out with this particular girl and her boyfriend. Nicole told her that she was fine, just a little tired. She said "Girl, I know the feeling". She said when she was pregnant, she was always tired. Nicole did not know why she said that but she let it go. The next time Nicole called the job, she asked Nicole about the pregnancy. Nicole asked her, "You think I am pregnant?" She said Ramon had told her that Nicole was pregnant. Nicole replied "He did?" When Ramon came to the phone, Nicole asked him about it. Of course, he told Nicole that he never told her anything like that.

About four months later, Nicole ran into a bus driver she and Ramon rode with every morning before they got their car. They greeted each other and he told Nicole that he ran into Ramon one day. He said "Congratulations". Nicole was confused and asked "For what?" He said "Your new bundle of joy". Nicole said "What bundle of joy?" He said

Ramon told him that Nicole had a baby. She told him that she did not have a baby. He said "Oh, maybe I heard wrong". They finished talking and he left. Nicole knew he did not hear wrong because the girl at Ramon's job thought she was pregnant also. "I couldn't understand why he would tell people I was pregnant. It scared me to know that he was capable of lying about something that important. But I always pushed back my worries by saying 'someday soon'.

"There always seemed to be a cloud of unhappiness hovering over us", Nicole sighed. "In the midst of Ramon's medical issues, we discovered that Ramon was not the only one with a medical problem." During Nicole's annual exam, she received some dreadful news. Fibroids. She was so shocked, she could not respond. The doctor proceeded to ask her "Nobody ever told you that you had fibroids?" Nicole replied, "NO". Dr. Orin then stated that she had a fibroid the size of a five month old baby. Again, all Nicole could say was "What?"

After she got dressed, she went into his office. Nicole said to the doctor, "I came to you last year and you never told me that I had fibroids." He asked her "You saw me?" She said "Yes, I did". He brushed it off by saying "Well I don't have your chart right now, so I don't know". Nicole thought to herself, why would a doctor check a person out without having their medical chart in front of him?

Dr. Orin told Nicole that he would schedule her to take a sonogram. She thought she would get an appointment in the mail. The appointment Nicole received was about two and a half weeks later. In the midst of her waiting for the sonogram, her mother told her to call the administration office and request a second opinion. Nicole called and they gave her an appointment to see Dr. Said at another GYN facility provided by her HMO. When Nicole got there, he examined her and had the nerve to say to her with an attitude, "Yes, you do have fibroids, what did you need a second opinion for?" Nicole told him because she could not believe she saw her doctor last year and he did not see anything.

He stated that it could grow that big in six months. He then told her to get dressed and just walked out of the room. This appointment lasted a good three minutes. She could not believe that the fibroids grew that big and no one saw anything. It was unbelievable to her because she never had any symptoms. She always heard that your menstrual would come down heavier or you would have bad cramps.

Everything was normal to Nicole. She just did not think that something so big did not cause any of these symptoms. But God is a good and merciful. Nicole did not think about it before but now she sees that all HMO doctors look out for each other. *"It is better to trust in the Lord than put your confidence in man"* Psalm 118:9.

Bishop White prayed for the members of the church one Sunday afternoon. When he got to Nicole, he said "Lord, don't let nothing be hidden in her body". As Nicole reflected back on that service, she believed God was revealing something was there. She may not have known the fibroids were there, but God knew. Another instance when the Lord spoke was when Evangelist Liston came over to speak to Nicole. She asked Nicole, "When was the last time you went to the doctor?" She told her that she went recently. She then asked Nicole, "What did they say?" Nicole replied that everything was well. She also asked Nicole, "Are you trying to get pregnant?" Nicole said "Yes". No one knew what Ramon and Nicole were going through. Nicole did not believe she wanted kids right then and there but she eventually wanted to start a family. The last thing Evangelist Liston said to Nicole was "The Lord is telling me to tell you to go back to the doctor".

God is so merciful. Nicole can see how God used these vessels to minister to her. A couple of weeks later, Nicole went to Flower Rise Hospital to take the sonogram. The technician told her dad that she had fibroids but they were not in the womb. Thank God for that! The word says "Be fruitful, and multiply". The technician told her that they were going to send her results to her doctor.

When Nicole got home, she called Dr. Orin to see if he could speed up the process. She wanted to take care of this problem quickly. She could not believe Dr. Orin would not get on the phone. The receptionist asked her what was it in reference to. She relayed the message back to the doctor. When she returned to the phone, she told Nicole "You just have to make an appointment. If it was that serious, they would have contacted the doctor already". They made her appointment for a month later. Nicole thought to herself, "Unbelievable!"

What made it so bad was that this appointment was only so Dr. Orin could tell her the results of the sonogram. That meant that she would have waited even longer for them to take care of the problem. Maybe Dr. Orin was upset because Nicole went for a second opinion. First, the doctor told her that she had something inside of her the size of a five month old baby, then he just brushed her off and gave her an appointment so far away. She could not believe her doctor seemed so uncaring. Then again, she could.

During the time of her waiting, she just prayed. *"Fear thou not; for I am with thee: be not dismayed; for I am thy God; I will strengthen thee; yea I will help thee; yea I will uphold thee with the right hand of my righteousness".* *Isaiah 41:10* Nicole thanked God for Ramon; he was really there for her. She thanked Ramon for his love, prayers, support, encouraging words and his quick thinking. Nicole believed God joined them together so that they could build each other up. Whenever Nicole was on the brink of a break down, Ramon always knew how to lift her up. Ramon has truly been a positive force in her life. She thanked him for the many nights that he prayed and labored over her.

She thanked God for her grandmother for all of her prayers, comfort and love. She also thanked God for her mother's prayers, comfort and love and for even accompanying her to her appointments. She also thanked God for her father. He was also very supportive. He went with her to a lot of her appointments. It was really cool because it brought her and Mr. Watts closer together. Her family had really been a blessing in her life. She loved her family with her whole heart. God knows, He could not have placed her with a better family.

One day Ramon called Nicole at work and said "Why don't you use my insurance and visit one of my doctors?" Nicole hesitated but said OK. He was always bragging about his doctor so she said to him "Can I see your doctor?" He said "Yes, that's a good idea". Ramon called his doctor on Friday and they made an appointment for Nicole to see him on that next Monday. Boy that was quick! She was used to HMO appointments being months away.

Ramon went with Nicole to see Dr. Stein. Dr. Stein was very nice and thorough. She could not believe it. He checked everything. When Nicole said everything she meant everything. Nicole's pressure was elevated because she was very nervous. She was always nervous when she went to the doctor. Nicole said that she was going to believe and wait on God to deliver her from that. Dr. Stein said "Your pressure is high and I am not going to let you leave here until it goes down." She could not believe what she was hearing. When she saw Dr. Jewels at her H.M.O. and her pressure was high, he just wanted to give her a pill and have her come back in two months. That is only one scenario.

Nicole saw the difference between private doctors and HMO doctors. When they checked the cardio machine, Nicole's heart was beating fast but normal. He wanted to make sure it was not anything serious so he had her wear a 24 hour heart monitor machine. Nicole had all these patches and this big monitor box hanging around her waist. The bad thing was that she had to go to work the next day. Nicole wore the biggest thing she could find to try and hide the wires and the machine. She was very successful.

Scenario #2 – When she went to Dr. Jewel's office her heart was beating fast and he told her "Its ok, you just have to lose weight because you are too heavy". Nicole took the machine back to Dr. Stein's office the next day. They said that the results would take at least one week. Dr. Stein also told her to call him the next day so he could refer her to a GYN doctor for the other problem.

The next day Ramon spoke to Dr. Stein for Nicole. Dr. Stein faxed him over a printout with a list of GYN doctors. Ramon made most of Nicole's phone calls because she did not have any privacy at her job. She did not get caught up in telling her co-workers her personal business. Ramon decided not to just pick a doctor but to go on the internet and find out their credentials. She knew that had to be God leading him. He called her and said that he found the doctor for her. He said his name was Dr. Jones and his office was in Queens, NY. He said he read Dr. Jones' profile and Dr. Jones had a lot of years of experience with gynecologic surgery. He was also on the New York Board of Physicians. Ramon stated that God had put in his spirit that this was the doctor for her. They called Dr. Jones office and made an appointment for two days later. Wow, Nicole thought that was fast.

Nicole went to see Dr. Jones. Before he took the sonogram, he asked her "Are you sure you are not pregnant?" Nicole replied "No, I am not pregnant." Nicole wouldn't dare tell the doctor that she never had sex with her husband. He then examined her and took a sonogram. Dr. Jones saw the fibroids and said that he could take them out. He wanted her to take another sonogram at another center. He told her to have them fax him the report. He felt their sonogram machine was more advanced. She was telling Dr. Jones about what was going on with her HMO. She did not know he was affiliated with HMO's at one time. He began to tell her that he did not like HMO's and had to get out of there. He said that HMO doctors like to take the easy way out. They would rather give you a hysterectomy and take your womb out rather than be careful and keep your womb intact.

Dr. Jones told her about a 21 year old girl that they wanted to give a hysterectomy. Her friend recommended her to Dr. Jones before it was too late. Can you imagine being 21 and never having kids? He gave her a myomectomy which means you are only removing the fibroids. The surgery was successful and she ended up having a baby. He then showed Nicole a picture of a little boy he called Little Fibroid. Dr. Jones told Nicole that he would perform the same surgery for her.

Scenario #3 – Private Doctors say I want to help you. I understand that you are only 21 and I want to see you have children. HMO doctors say I don't care how old you are and frankly I could care less whether you have children or not. This is the procedure that you have to have. It is much easier for me to take everything out than for me to have to be careful in a surgery.

Nicole called into work late and went to take the sonogram the next morning. She also requested that they fax the report to Dr. Jones. Dr. Jones' assistant called her the next day. She wanted to know if Nicole wanted to schedule the surgery for this month or next month. She told her that she wanted to schedule it for this month. She wanted those fibroids out of her. Linda told her that someone from Saint Mary's Hospital would call her with an appointment date. Don't you know; they called while Nicole was not home and left a message for her to call them. When Nicole called, they scheduled her surgery for that month. She could not believe it.

In the midst of Nicole waiting for the surgery date, Dr. Stein called her house. He told her that he wanted her to make an appointment to see a cardiologist named Dr. Weinburg. The appointment was for the end of the month. He works at the same office. He wanted Nicole to take an echocardiogram. Her dad went with her of course. Somebody had to be there. Nicole took the echocardiogram and then went back to work. They said it would take a week to get the results.

Two days before the surgery, Nicole had to go to Saint Mary's Hospital for the pre-surgery screening. They took her blood, checked her heart, took chest x-rays, asked a couple of questions and she filled out some forms. She thanked God everything was ok. They would not have let Nicole go through with the surgery otherwise.

It was now the day of the surgery. Nicole had to be there at 6:30am. Ramon and Mrs. Watts went with Nicole to the hospital. When they got there, she had to sign some papers. The nurse told Nicole to go into the bathroom and change her clothes. She had to change into a robe and slippers. She was a little nervous. When she came out the bathroom, she had to sit there and wait for Dr. Jones to call her in. Remember earlier when Nicole said that the HMO center scheduled her appointment for the end of the month? Well, that date came and went. No one from the office called or sent her a letter concerning her sonogram. To this day, Nicole still had not heard from them.

There was a lady there named Diane. Her friend Tanya was having surgery also. Nicole did not know Diane from a hole in the wall but she asked her "What kind of surgery are you having?" She did not even care that Ramon was standing there. Mrs. Watts went out to use the phone. She guessed the look on Nicole's face said "None of your business". She then said "One of those female things". Nicole just said "Yes". She should have been trying to comfort her friend rather than trying to be in her business.

While Nicole was waiting to be called, the anesthesiologist came out to speak to Nicole, Ramon and Mrs. Watts. He was telling them about the procedure. When he was finished, Ramon and Mrs. Watts said "Please take care of my baby". He then stated, "Your baby is going to be fine". Nicole was so happy they came with her. She must admit, she acts like a baby at times.

The nurse at the front desk told Ramon and Mrs. Watts that they had to sit in the waiting area. The nurse told them that they should come back around 5:00pm. She said that she should be out of surgery by then. Ramon and Mrs. Watts said that they would be in the waiting area. They were not going to leave until she actually went into surgery. Whenever a doctor or whoever came to speak to her, Nicole ran to the door and got Ramon and Mrs. Watts so they could hear everything that was going on.

Nicole was sitting down thinking and praying. She began to thank God for how everything was working out. There was a pastor by the name of Wendy Johnson who came to Nicole and Ramon's church to preach. Her text came from Ruth 3:1-7. She said that God told her that there was going to be unbelievable favor in this month of May. Ramon and Nicole took that word and stood fast to God's promises. Nicole was thinking about that and other messages she heard regarding healing, favor and deliverance. It was really getting cold in the room.

There was a gentleman who came around and put a blanket over everyone that was cold. While they waited, Tanya began to have a small talk with Nicole. She did not want to cut her off because maybe she could encourage Tanya and herself in some way. All she was talking about was "It is cold in here". I wish they would call us. Who is your doctor?" When she told her who her doctor was, she said her doctor is Dr. Welch. Nicole did not know what made her tell Nicole her next sentence because she did not ask her. She said "I am not having a hysterectomy". It came out of left field because they were not talking about that. Nicole did not know if she was waiting for her to tell her what kind of procedure she was having. Nicole kept her wondering. Nicole did not say a word about what she was having.

After the anesthesiologist spoke to them, a female doctor who was going to be assisting Dr. Jones came and spoke to them. While she was talking to them, she said something that Nicole did not want to hear. She started off by introducing herself and then she went into a subject that made Nicole burst out into tears. She said "For life threatening measures, if you start to hemorrhage, we would have to give you a hysterectomy".

Nicole could not stop the tears from coming. Ramon started saying "Nicole, what did we talk about? Stop worrying, God is in control". Mrs. Watts was saying "Nicole, you are not going to have a hysterectomy. Nicole, you can't act like that. You have to show faith in God". They were saying a lot of encouraging things but Nicole was too out of it by then to hear anything.

After the female doctor came with the bad news, another doctor came in. By that time she was already crying. He said "I don't know what she told you but this is what we are going to do". He was basically telling them about the surgery. Nicole then told him what the other doctor told her. He said that they have to tell you that just in case something was to happen. He told Nicole not to worry because it happens once out of every thousand people. While he was speaking to them, Dr. Jones came out and said "I'm ready". When he looked at her face, he said "No crying in my room". Ramon and Mrs. Watts started telling Dr. Jones "Please take care of my baby". Nicole believed Ramon even hugged Dr. Jones. Dr. Jones said "Don't worry; she is going to be alright".

The third doctor asked Nicole if she had to use the restroom before she went into surgery. She said "Yes". When she got in there she just began to pray and ask God to please let everything work out fine. ***"But he was wounded for our transgressions; he was bruised for our iniquities: the chastisement of our peace was upon him; and with his stripes we are healed." Isaiah 53:5.*** She came out the bathroom and told the doctor "I am ready". Nicole could not believe she said that. She was walking out the bathroom like a champ.

Mrs. Watts told Nicole later that she was amazed she came out the bathroom like that. She was wondering what happened in the bathroom. Now that Nicole thinks about it, God quickened her spirit and revealed to her that all was well. Nicole gave Ramon and her mother a kiss and went into the surgery room.

Ramon revealed to Nicole later that Dr. Jones told them to come back at a quarter to eleven. Mind you, she went into the surgery at 9:30am. Nicole guessed the front desk nurse did not know what she was talking about when she told them to come back at 5:00pm.

Nicole remembers walking into the surgery room. The big champ that walked out of the bathroom turned into a medium size champ. She saw all of these big machines. Everything looked white. Do you know that song "Heaven is mine?" Well, Nicole knows Heaven is hers but she did not want to go right then and there. Dr. Jones was not in the room yet. Nicole was waiting for them to give her the anesthesia. Then a gentleman said to her "Hi, my name is James" and a big, tall lady said "Hi, my name is Janet". She said "Hello, my name is Nicole". Janet told Nicole to sit on the table. As Nicole was walking towards the table a third voice said "Think of something good. Think about what you want to do when you get out of here".

Nicole went to sit on the table and of course she laid the wrong way. Janet said "the other way". Nicole said, "I'm sorry", like she was going to beat her up for sitting the wrong way. She said "It's OK". When she laid down, the same guy who told her to think about something good, told her to put her left arm out. She saw him getting ready to give her a needle and that was the last thing she remembered.

Nicole did not remember going to the recovery room. She only remembered waking up in her room. Ramon once told Nicole about the story when he went for surgery. He said that he was coming out of the anesthesia and he thought that they were still performing the surgery. He started yelling "I am waking up, I am waking up". Everybody started laughing at him because the surgery was over hours before.

Well, Nicole also had a similar story about when she was coming out of the anesthesia. When they brought Nicole up to her room, they were trying to wake her up so she could move from one bed to another. Could you imagine just coming out of surgery and they want you to pull yourself over. All she could say is pain, pain and more pain. She remembers yelling "Should I be getting up, should I be getting up?" They said "yes, you are in your room now." When Nicole thought about their similar situations, she could not help but laugh.

Nicole was out of it the first day. She thought she slept more than anything. She remembers waking up one time and her room was full of people. She was so happy to see everybody. They brought balloons, flowers and teddy bears. It was so nice of them to do that for her. Then she was out again. Ramon said he thought she woke up every hour for maybe a minute. She did remember waking up for some pain killers and telling Ramon not to leave her. Although visiting hours were over at 8:00pm, they let Ramon sit with her until 10:00pm. She had to admit, the nurses were very nice. Not one of them came in there with a nasty attitude. She also remembered her legs vibrating.

She did not know what it was. Nicole asked Ramon and he told her that it was used to increase circulation in her legs since she was not walking.

On the second day, Nicole was feeling a lot better. Do you remember the doctor that gave Nicole the news about the possibility of having a hysterectomy? Well anyway, she came into her room and asked how she was doing. She told her "I still have a little pain but it was not as bad as the first day". She then asked Nicole if she wanted a picture of the fibroids. She told her "Yes". She told her that she would give it to her later and left the room. She never brought it to her that day but it was ok because Mrs. Watts ended up showing Nicole her picture. Dr. Jones gave Mrs. Watts a picture of the fibroids when the surgery was over.

The nurse came into the room and removed the tube that was used to urinate in. They also took that vibrating machine off of Nicole. She told Nicole that she wanted her to try and walk. It seemed not long after she removed the tube out of her that Nicole had to use the bathroom. So, Nicole had to finally get out of the bed and use the bathroom. Ramon helped Nicole get out of the bed. All she could feel was pain, pain and more pain. It took her three minutes to get to the bathroom which was in the same room. After she used the bathroom, she got right back in the bed.

Nicole was happy again because her room was packed with visitors. Nicole felt bad for the lady in the next bed. She kept moaning, groaning and complaining about the pain.

Nicole was not sure what type of surgery she had but she was in a lot of pain. The nurse told Nicole that she had to walk around. She told her that walking to the bathroom and back to her bed is not going to help.

Nicole finally decided that she was going to walk. Ramon and Nicole took a long walk all the way to the end of the hall. On their way back and towards the other end, they heard someone saying "Hello, how are you?" When they looked, it was Diane. They said hello back. Nicole looked in the room and saw Tanya sleeping. She asked her how she was doing. She gave Nicole a look as to say, I guess she's alright. She then told Ramon and Nicole something that Tanya would have been mad about.

She said "You know my friend had a hysterectomy". Nicole did not remember what she said after that because she was in a state of shock. She could not believe what she heard. Do you remember earlier in my story I told you that Tanya said she was not having a hysterectomy? Ramon and Nicole continued to walk. While they were walking, Nicole just began to tell Ramon about the story. Nicole was wondering if she lied to her about not getting a hysterectomy or was she the one in a thousand people that had to get it for life threatening measures. They just began to thank and praise God as they were walking. It seemed like Nicole was a pro now because she did not want to get back in the bed. She still had a little pain but she still wanted to walk.

They walked another lap and a half. Ramon told Nicole "That's enough, get back in the bed". After a little while in the bed, Nicole decided that she wanted to sit in the chair. She sat in the chair for a while and later got back in the bed. The time was then 8:00pm. Security started telling everyone to leave. Ramon and Nicole gave everyone a kiss and said goodnight. That night they let Ramon stay until 10:30pm.

After Ramon left, Nicole turned off the television and started to read her bible. The lady next to her was still moaning. She tried to take as much pain as she could because she did not want to get hooked on the pain killers. Nicole told her to call her nurse and ask her for some pain killers. She said that it was not time. She was already given medicine to ease the pain. Nicole thought her pain rubbed off on her because her stomach started hurting. Nicole was very uncomfortable.

Nicole got out of the bed and sat in the chair. She felt so much better sitting up. The nurse would come in their room in the middle of the night and check their pressure and give them pain killers if they needed it. When she came in the room, she did not see Nicole in the bed. Nicole said to her "I am right here". She started laughing and said "Oh, I thought you ran away". Nicole told her that she felt much better sitting up than lying down. She checked her pressure, gave her a pill. Nicole ended up sleeping in that chair the rest of the night.

By the third day, Nicole was getting around pretty good. She was sitting on the chair and had her feet on the bed. The nurse came in and told her that she could take a shower. Before Nicole went to take her shower, the doctor came in and brought her the picture that her mother already showed her. She then told Nicole that when she gets pregnant, she suggests that she have a cesarean. She also told her that the fibroids could grow back. When she said it, it did not bother Nicole. *"For I will restore health unto thee, and I will heal thee of thy wounds, saith the Lord."* *Jeremiah 30:17*

God gave Nicole peace. God had everything under control so the enemy had to send someone to try and discourage her. That doctor had been the only negative force since the beginning of the operation. Nicole told God that she was leaving it in his hands and she went down the hall to take her shower.

When Nicole came back from the shower, she sat in the chair with her feet on the bed. Dr. Jones walked in and asked her how she was doing. She jumped on her feet and gave him the biggest hug. She kept saying "Thank you doctor". Although she knew it was God that performed the surgery, she wanted to thank the doctor that God used. He saw how she was getting around so he asked her if she wanted to go home. Nicole told him "If you think I am well enough, sure ". He told her that he would fill out her discharge forms. He told her that he wanted her to come to his office in the next two weeks. He gave her a prescription for antibiotics and pain killers. Nicole thanked him again and he left.

After Dr. Jones left, she called Ramon at home and told him that the doctor was releasing her and that he had to bring her some clothes. Ramon went shopping and brought Nicole a big bag of stuff. He even brought her a pack of underwear for a 500 pound woman. He laughed and said that he did not look at the size.

Immediately after the surgery, Nicole could not eat any solid foods. They had her on a liquid diet. The first day, she had the I.V. in her arm. The second and third day she had milk, broth, ice cream, pudding, fruit cups etc. She had liquid foods for breakfast, lunch and dinner. The good thing about it was that she did not feel hungry.

Ramon came to the hospital around 9:30am. He started to help her get her stuff together. Nicole started to put her clothes on. The lady next to her was still in pain. Nicole reflected on her progress in comparison and silently thanked the Lord again. She told her neighbor to feel better and take care and then she and Ramon went to the front desk and signed the release forms. All the nurses were saying "You are walking good. Take care". Ramon and Nicole began to tell them how nice they were. They also told them that they had made Nicole's stay a very comfortable one. They then left and went home.

It felt so good to be home. Nicole thought to herself that it was good to be in her own bed. Ramon treated Nicole like a queen. He took the whole week off from work plus a few days every week after that. Nicole's dad, Mr. Watts came over and cooked for her. Her mom came over and cooked for her. Her grandma also came over and cooked for her. Her friend Ebony stayed with her a few days. Even her nephew Donald stayed with her one day. He talked her to death but she enjoyed his company. She thanked God for the many phone calls and visitors.

There is nothing like feeling loved! "This was another time in our marriage when I thought that everything would work out for us, Nicole said. My husband was being everything I had been taught a husband should be. My protector, my friend, my covering.....it seemed as though our love was growing deeper, in spite of the things that still hadn't worked out yet."

While Nicole was home, she built a closer relationship with the Lord. She thought that she needed that time to get closer to the Lord. ***It is good for me that I have been afflicted; that I might learn thy statues."*** *Psalms 119:71.* When you work every day and have to come home and cook and clean, you tend to slack up on your time with God. But Nicole learned through this ordeal that God comes first no matter what. While they were home together Ramon and Nicole woke up with a praise of thanksgiving on their lips. They prayed and got into the word together on a daily basis. God is a merciful and faithful God.

Dr. Stein called Ramon's job and told him that he wanted Nicole to make an appointment to see Dr. Weinburg. Remember, Nicole was still waiting for the results of the echocardiogram. He told Ramon and Nicole that the echocardiogram came back normal. He said that Nicole just had an accelerated heartbeat. He also said that her heart was a regular size and the blood was flowing equally through the different organs. He said that there was nothing seriously wrong. Hallelujah! When they went back to his office, he stated that Nicole needed to lose weight. He said that could be the cause of her heart beating fast. She was happy that she at least lost six pounds since she was in the hospital.

When Nicole first went to Dr. Stein's office, she weighed two hundred fourteen pounds. She just covered it up well with the clothes she wore. After the surgery, she went down to 208. Nicole did not lose much but it was a start. Nicole would not serve another God. *"And ye shall serve the Lord your God, and he shall bless thy bread, and thy water; and I will take sickness away from the midst of thee."* Exodus 23:25

Nicole went back to Dr. Jones office in two weeks. The nurse could not believe how well she was walking. She said that people usually walk in there bent over and in pain after surgery. Dr. Jones told Nicole to lie on the bed. She went to lay down straight back and laid back to fast. Boy was she in pain. He checked the incision. He said that everything looked good. He told her to make another appointment in two weeks.

When Nicole went to the next appointment, he checked everything and said everything looked good. He said that her womb was intact and in excellent condition. He pressed down on her stomach a few times and checked the incision. After he examined everything, they went back to his office. He told her that the fibroids weighed more than one pound, WOW! He told Nicole that she was well enough to go back to work. He told her to just rest for two weeks and then go back. Nicole asked him if she had to make another appointment to see him and he said "Yes", when you get pregnant". She wanted to shout but she had to keep her composure until she got outside. She asked him if she could go to church and he said yes. She told Dr. Jones that she would see him later and then she left. Nicole was excited about going back to church.

Nicole saw God's hand in everything that occurred. God had everything planned out. How could there not have been any symptoms that this thing was inside of her? God watches over and keeps his own. Before Ramon got his job, Nicole was trying to get him a job with her company in the Law Department. Nicole gave her co-worker the resume that she typed up for Ramon. That meant that Ramon and Nicole would have had the same health insurance.

That is only one reason why he did not hear from them. God knew exactly when Ramon and Nicole should have gotten married. What if they were not married? No matter what happens in life, it happens for a reason. Nicole would've had to deal with her H.M.O., the same people who did not respond yet. As big as the fibroids were, she was quite sure they would have told her that she had to have a hysterectomy.

What about Tanya? Did she know that she had to have that surgery? What if the surgery did not go well and they had to give her a hysterectomy? I mentioned earlier about unbelievable favor. Well, the favor that God placed in Nicole's life was unbelievable. *"Many are the afflictions of the righteous: but the Lord delivereth them out of them all" Psalm 34:19*

There is a nurse that works at Freeport Hospital. She has been a friend of Nicole's family for many years. Her mother showed her the picture of the fibroids and she could not believe what she was seeing. She told Nicole's mother that they should seek legal counseling. She said that they should have seen something last year.

Nicole's grandmother told her to just leave it alone. She said to just thank God that He delivered her out of this bad situation. She said that she should just move on and start her new life. She said to just keep her mind on Christ. Nicole decided to take her grandmother's advice.

God has been good to Nicole. When Nicole would think of the goodness of Jesus and all that He had done for her, her soul cried out, "Hallelujah". She thanked God for delivering, healing and keeping her.

God is an on time God. You have to realize that the way has already been made for you. You have to make up your mind that you are coming out. God will order your steps and direct your path. Cast all your cares upon the Lord for He cares for you. Remember, the devil is a liar. He walks around seeking whom he may devour. Resist the devil and he will flee. God has not brought you this far to turn his back on you now. *"No weapon that is formed against you shall prosper".* Isaiah 54:17. You have to hold fast to God's word without wavering. It is impossible to please God without faith.

After Nicole came home from the hospital, Ramon and Nicole talked about how much they wanted kids. She figured with Ramon going to the doctor and she just having her surgery, they could now try and have a baby. The doctor told her that she had to wait six weeks before she should have sex. Since they seemed to have drawn closer during this difficult time Ramon and Nicole were hopeful that, once the waiting period was over, they could finally be fully intimate with one another. Unfortunately, that didn't happen. Ramon was still unable to perform.

One day, Ramon told Nicole that he was going downtown to take the State Bar exam. He said that there were two parts to the test. Part one was on one day and part two was on another. Nicole asked Ramon how he thought he did. He said that he thought he messed up on one part but he thinks he passed it. After months had passed, Nicole asked Ramon if he found out the results. Unfortunately on September 11, 2001 the United States of America was attacked by terrorist. The World Trade Center was one of the places hit. Ramon told Nicole that he could not get the result of the State Bar exam because the office was inside the World Trade center. That was such a coincidence. He said that the Bar was given twice a year and that if he didn't get the results, he would have to take the test over. He said that he was going to wait at least six months to give him time to study.

On September 11, 2001, Ramon told Nicole that he was on the 94th floor in the World Trade Center building #2. That was where the first plane hit. He said that his boss booked the room but they gave the room to someone else. He said they argued for a while then left. When they got out of the building, the first plane hit. The next thing Nicole knew, he said they ended up in Jersey at the main office for his company. He said that he had to stay out there over night. He kept calling Nicole from a Jersey number which was supposed to be a hotel. He came home the next day and began to tell Nicole about his experience.

One Sunday after September 11, Nicole recalls Bishop White calling everyone up to the front of the church who was in the World Trade Center when the planes hit. He was thanking God that no one was lost in the church. Deacon Desmond and Ramon ran to the front of the church and the whole entire church went up in praise.

Chapter 5

I Don't Love You Any More

One day Ramon came home talking about how he felt for the first time in his life, that he did not have to struggle. He was still supposed to be paying back his school loan. Weeks later, Nicole went to buy some sneakers. Ramon saw some boots he liked so she said to him, "Why don't you buy them?" (Ramon had told Nicole that he does not have to struggle anymore.) He just said, "I don't need the boots that bad, I'll wait".

Ramon and Nicole were talking one day and he said that he did not want to be a lawyer. He said that he would rather work at the bank. He said that he had a better opportunity of making more money working at the bank. He said that he was closing some big deals. Nicole said to him "Why don't you want to be a lawyer?" You went to school all this time and you want to give up on your dreams"? He said "Why can't you be supportive? I said I don't want to be a lawyer". Nicole said to him "Well, it's up to you." She left it at that.

Ramon began to tell Nicole that he did not want to be touched. Ramon went to the doctor a few times without Nicole. He said that he was just going to go there and go straight to work. He said that she did not have to go with him. She didn't believe he went to the doctor. He said that he was tired of doctors touching him. He just did not want to be touched by anyone. She went to see their family doctor one day and she asked him about Ramon. He said that all of Ramon's tests came back normal. He said that even with the under developed testicle and the heightened penis, everything seemed normal. He said that his blood tests were fine. He could not understand why he was having a problem getting an erection. Ramon was also prescribed some Viagra which he claimed did not work either.

Nicole told Ramon that she felt that they should speak to Bishop. They scheduled a meeting. When they got there, Ramon began telling him everything. He even told their Bishop that he did not want to be like his sister Sandra and her husband Jacob. Ramon said that he felt Jacob was robbing Sandra of a happy life. He felt that Jacob should have let her go because he knew how bad she wanted kids. He told their Bishop that Jacob was being selfish. Ramon and Nicole used to talk about kids a lot. He said that he knew how bad Nicole wanted kids.

Ramon wanted Nicole to leave him. He felt Nicole would be happy with someone else who could give her what he could not give her. Nicole told Bishop that she thought it had to do with another woman. Bishop said that he thought Nicole should get that out of her mind. He said that if Ramon could not please Nicole, how was he going to please someone else? Ramon was so excited that Bishop said that he responded by saying "Thank you Bishop, thank you Bishop".

Bishop spoke to them a long time. He asked Ramon how he could say that he loved Nicole since he was thirteen years old and doesn't love her now. At the end of the conversation, Bishop asked her if she was willing to try and make it work. Nicole said "Yes". He asked Ramon and he said "I have to think about it Bishop". Bishop said "Well, he did not say no". They then left the church and went home. While they were driving, it was really quiet in the car. Nicole began to make conversation. Things seemed to be ok. Ramon's reasoning for feeling the way he was feeling was because he did not want to be like his sister and her husband.

Nicole wanted to see if she was right about how she was feeling. (Nicole suspected it was another woman) She went down to Ramon's job without him knowing. Nicole saw Ramon play fighting with a Spanish girl. She later found out that she was twenty years old. Nicole could not believe what she was seeing. The same guy who did not want to be touched was play fighting and carrying on with another woman. She walked up to the window and told Ramon to come outside. You should have seen the look on their faces. She looked like she was scared so she started to play fight with another female co-worker. She looked so stupid because the girl was looking at her as if to say, "Hey, I was not playing with you". Ramon looked very nervous. He came outside saying, "There is nothing going on. Please don't embarrass me.", he pleaded. He claimed he was not messing around with her, they were just playing around.

Nicole kept telling her to come outside. But she was too scared. Nicole asked Ramon her name and he said Vicki. Eventually she had to come outside because they were closing the bank. Nicole approached Vicki and asked her what was going on. She said "Nothing, we are just friends". Vicki said that she plays with everyone like that. Nicole told her that she did not want her playing with Ramon like that.

Nicole asked him what her last name was and he said "Lopez". (She remembered Ramon called a V. Lopez on the house phone when she was not there.) She said "Oh that is the same person you were calling from the house phone." He said that he was calling a Victor Lopez from his job to see if he could work overtime. She told Ramon that he was lying. Nicole knew that Vicki was the person he had been calling. Nicole got so upset that she started walking ahead of him. Ramon could not even please and consummate with his wife but you would be playing around with another woman. She even started yelling at him in the street which is something she had never done before.

He got tired of her mouth so he said to her "Well, how do you know it is a woman?" She turned and looked at him and said "Don't tell me you are gay." He said "No, I am not gay". Nicole asked why he said that. He did not answer Nicole. Then she started seeing Vicki Lopez in his cell phone. Every time Nicole would erase the number, he would put it back. She used to call the job and Vicki would say "Hi Nicole, let me get your husband". Ramon had the nerve to tell Nicole that Vicki liked her a lot and thought Nicole was a very nice person.

Ramon had started hanging out late. He would tell Nicole that he did not want to come home and see her disappointed with him. Nicole would call his cell phone and he would not answer. He went from not wanting to be like Jacob and Sandra to Nicole not being supportive of him. When he would come home, he would sleep in the living room. He did not want to sleep in the same bed with Nicole. He would act like he was watching television in the living room and stay in there. Ramon had always been sensitive to Nicole's needs. Now, Nicole could not pay him to care. Nicole did not know what was becoming of Ramon. He told Nicole that he did not love her but he cared about what happened to her. He said that he felt more like Nicole's best friend than her husband.

Ramon kept telling Nicole that he had to leave. He said that she was not supportive. He said that he was there for her when she was in the hospital. Ramon felt Nicole was not there for him when he was going through his problem. How was Nicole not there for him when she encouraged him to go to the doctor and take care of his problem? Also, she never went outside the marriage and cheated on him. Mind you, while he was going through his problem, she was the one praying for him. She could have been with someone else since he could not perform. She was faithful to the man. Nicole said some things that she regrets. She told him that she did not wish him on anyone. Nicole kept asking "God, why me?" She began to put the blame on herself until she realized that Ramon was the cause of the problem.

Ramon continued to tell Nicole that he wanted to leave. One day, Nicole got so fed up with him that she decided to scare him. She figured if she scared him, he would stop talking about leaving. Ramon kept threatening to leave her after she stayed by his side all this time even though he could not perform. Nicole, filled with rage, went into the kitchen and got a knife. She told him that she was tired of him saying that he was going to leave.

While Ramon was sitting on the couch, Nicole was standing by the door way with a knife. "You think after all this time I've spent standing by YOUR side, even when I was miserable that you are going to leave me? You think that after how I've covered up for you and your lies and excuses that you're going to walk out on me?? You think that after I've been cheated out of a happy marriage and a normal sex life that you get to call it quits?? After I spent time in prayer that you would be healed, you're telling me that you are leaving? I GET TO CALL IT QUITS!! Not you!" she yelled at the top of her lungs. Ramon was really scared and he had the pillow in front of his chest. He kept saying, "Nicole, please let's pray about this. We can work everything out." She said to him "Oh, you want to pray now; well, I don't want to pray". Nicole acted as if she had lost her mind. After a while, Nicole got tired of the crazy game so she acted like she was willing to pray about it with Ramon. Ramon walked over to Nicole and took the knife out of her hands. He pleaded with a trembling voice, "Come on, let's get on our knees and pray now".

When they finished praying, Nicole got up and went into the bathroom. She took the cordless phone with her. Nicole called her mother and grandmother laughing. She was telling them what happened. Nicole knew it was wrong but she felt like she needed to scare him. Nicole's grandmother and mother were very upset about what she did and told her that it was not right. I wonder what made Nicole call them because she knew they were the last people that were going to agree with her. (Nicole was far from crazy.)

She knew if she would have stabbed someone, Big Janet would have been running after her in jail. Obviously, this trick did not work because Ramon left anyway. It actually made matters worse. Ramon ended up using this incident against her later on in the story. Nicole, looked at me while I was thinking about the "crazy episode" and said sadly "I think about that night sometimes now and realize how much I wanted to hang on to my fake life. I was so used to him just being around me that I didn't know what life would be like if he weren't there. I was so used to pretending to be the happy couple that I guess in some way I believed my own fake life." Nicole looked at me and I looked at her. There was really nothing else to say.

Ramon left on his birthday. The day he left was the day Nicole showed up at my house to tell me her terribly sad story. The day he left was the day I realized that my friend had been deceived. The day he left was the day that I realized that I had been deceived too. I had to admit to myself that all this time I had actually been envious of Nicole and her marriage. And I had to admit that I had been feeling like God had cheated me by blessing her with a husband instead of me. What a deception!!

All this time I should have been praying for my friend. And all this time I should have realized that what God has for me is for me and that things aren't always what they seem. Yes, street smart Sabrina had been deceived too. Have you ever been deceived about the struggles of the people in your life or the sovereignty of God? Think about it.

Ramon went to stay at his dad's house. Nicole later found out that he barely stayed there. She had planned a nice evening for them. They were going to go out that night. She had all his presents lying out on the couch. Nicole wanted to surprise him. Ramon told her that he would be home at 6:30pm. Well 6:30 came, 9:30 came, 1:00am came and Ramon never came home. Nicole ended up falling asleep on the love chair. She woke up the next morning and Ramon still was not home. He had been coming home late in the past few weeks but he never stayed out all night.

She called her mother and Mrs. Watts called Elder Williams. Ramon was at his father's house in Queens. Nicole and her mother rode out to Queens to see what happened. When they got there, Ramon came down stairs. Nicole noticed he was not wearing his ring. Mrs. Watts began to ask him what was wrong. He started to say what he had been saying about Nicole. He said that she was not there for him etc. He said that he just needed a little time away.

Ramon told Mrs. Watts about the time Nicole had the knife. He thought that Mrs. Watts did not know about it. Ramon said "Ma, I bet she did not tell you about the knife incident". He felt low when she said "Yes, she told me about it". Ramon began to say that Nicole scared him really bad. The only one surprised about the incident was Elder Williams. Nicole never told Ramon that it was done to scare him.

He said that he was going to stay at his father's house. Ramon decided to have his father bring him up to the Bronx to get some of his clothes. When they got there, Ramon and Carlton came upstairs. His father stayed in the car. Nicole did the unthinkable. She began to cry and begged him to stay. She told him that he should stay because it was the enemy trying to separate them. (At times when Nicole would look back on this entire ordeal, she would feel like an idiot.) "What woman would want to stay with a man that couldn't perform", she sobbed. "I guess when you are raised in a Christian family and taught to value marriage through good and bad times, you try and stick it out." Ramon began to tell her that he was only going to be gone for a week. He said, "See Nicole, I did not take all my clothes." He just took about five suits. Ramon began to hold his head like he was crying saying "I don't know what to do. Should I stay even with the way that I am feeling? Should I leave? I don't know what to do. I need help. I need a psychiatrist."

Nicole wanted him to get help so she made an appointment for Tuesday. When Ramon finished packing, he gave Nicole a kiss and a hug. She told him that she was not going to walk him to the door because she did not want to see him leave. He told her alright. He said that is why he wanted to get his things when she was not home. Nicole knows that is not the only reason he wanted to come to the house while she was not home. Ramon finally left.

At that point, Ramon was gone a while. No one from the church knew Nicole and Ramon were separated. If they knew, they sure did not ask her any questions. Nicole felt like a failure and was too ashamed to let anyone know what she was going through. She started going to church when she knew service started and she would walk out before it was over. She was dodging questions. Nicole recalled running into a member on the street and she said to Nicole, "Hey Nicole. How are you? I saw Ramon one day standing at a bus stop near my home. He didn't seem like himself and he was wearing some old fashioned clothes". Nicole found out later that Ramon was wearing Vicki's deceased uncle's clothes.

That same weekend Ramon left was the same weekend he and Nicole had planned to go to Pennsylvania with the family. Nicole's sister was christening her goddaughter. Ramon had already told Nicole that he did not want to go. She asked him why he did not want to go and he said because it was for the weekend. Mrs. Watts asked him and he told her that his job was sending him on a business trip.

Nicole went to Pennsylvania anyway with her family. They had a good time. They even went to Felder's Amusement Park. They went to visit a church there on Sunday and after the preacher finished his sermon he called people up for prayer. Mrs. Watts told Nicole to go up to the altar. Nicole told her no. Nicole ended up walking up there anyway. When the Pastor looked at Nicole he began to say "Let me tell you something, God is telling me to tell you that no weapon that is formed against you shall prosper. God said your brighter days are before you. God said don't even let the enemy take it back into memory. God said he has already put it inside of you. He is birthing in you a new direction and a new anointing.

God said, You haven't seen nothin' yet. Things are falling into place in your life. I don't even know you. But some things have been rough and you feel like giving up. God said keep swimming in it. God said to speak those things that are not as though they are. You have to start speaking things into your life. God said that you are more than a conqueror. The battle is not yours but it is the Lords." He asked God to bless her from the crown of her head to the sole of her feet. "Renew a right spirit in her. Do it for her now God," he said. All Nicole could do was cry and cry. God knew what she was about to go up against.

Chapter 6

Behind The Mask

A t this point in her life, Nicole was home alone. Ramon was still gone and she felt like she was calling him five hundred times a day. While he was gone, Nicole began to go through his things. You would not believe what she found. She found Ramon's school transcript from Gateway University. He went to Gateway for four and a half years. His grades were horrible. His last semester, he did not get anything higher than a D. Nicole called Gateway University to verify if he graduated or not. The person she spoke to said that she could not give her any information but she could tell her that he did not graduate. She explained that he still had a balance from the school.

Nicole's brother called Shoreway University and they told him that they do not have anyone by that name that has ever attended that school. Nicole could not believe it. She found a fake degree that he had made up in the computer. It looked exactly like Nicole's except that it did not have the seal or the signatures. The school he made the degree out for was Gateway University. Now what happened to Shoreway University?

Nicole recalls one Sunday at church when Ramon told Bishop White that he was graduating from Law School. Bishop had the entire congregation stand up and applaud Ramon. Everyone started screaming and yelling. They were so excited about how God was blessing Ramon. They really celebrated his accomplishments. Ramon told her that his position at his current job was a Legal Analyst and that he said he wrote up wills for bank customers.

Nicole found out that he was only a Customer Service Representative. She should have known because he sat in the front of the bank along with the other customer service representatives. She found the resume she had typed up for him. The resume she typed did not mention anything about Gateway University. Everything had to do with Shoreway University. She even asked him about his high school diploma. He told her that it was at his parent's house. She found his diploma with the rest of his papers at their house. His pay check stubs stated that he only made $12.13 an hour. She remembers playing with Ramon saying "I make more money than you." He just kept saying no you don't. Little did she know; she was right.

He used to get mad when she would tell him how good her credit was. He would tell her to switch places with him. He said if he was not in school, he would be able to buy a house, car etc. He complained about how much money he gave Gateway and Shoreway Universities. Nicole found a box of checks that had both of their names on it. Nicole thought Ramon and she worked together financially but she never opened up a bank account with him. Also, he filled out some application for his job to try and get reimbursed for the money he paid for school.

He told Nicole that they were going to pay for him to go to school. Ramon had stopped going to school four years ago. He even had the classes listed on the form. She found old check stubs from his previous job. His rate of pay was $9.18 an hour. He used a pen and wrote a number two in front of the 9 so it looked like he brought home $29.18 an hour. He received many forms stating that he did not have sufficient funds in his account to pay for the checks he wrote. She found a beneficiary form from his job that he filled out. The funny thing was he did not even have Nicole's name listed as one of the beneficiaries. Only his mother's name was listed.

Nicole and her mother went to the bank. Nicole told them that she did not sign for any checks to be made in her name. The customer service representative looked the information up in the computer. She said that she could not give her any information because her name was not on that account. A week later, Nicole's brother Edward took her to another branch. He told them that Nicole wanted to find out what was going on with that account. The rep took the check and pulled up the information. She said that one of the banks was not paying for the checks that Nicole wrote. Nicole did not want to tell her that she did not write the checks. She just let her say whatever she wanted to say. She wanted to find out what was going on. She gave Nicole a printout of what was going on in that account. It appears that Ramon was check kiting. He was writing checks from his account that was closed from another bank and putting it into his current account where he worked. He would take the money out of the bank before the check cleared. How crazy was that?

Nicole contacted the fraud department because she did not want to be liable for anything he was doing. They would not give Nicole any information because her name was not in the computer. Nicole kept calling anyway. She finally contacted the CEO's office and explained the situation to them. They told her that they were going to look into it and contact her later. Nicole told them that she wanted a letter from them stating that her name is not on the account and she will not be liable for anything that happens. They told her that once the account was closed they would give her a letter.

One day, Nicole decided to stay home because she just did not feel like going to work. The phone rang. The person said "Let me speak to Ramon". Nicole asked "Who is this?" She said "Diana from 1-800-Flowers". Nicole told her that he was not at home. Ramon never checked the email. He would always leave it up to Nicole to check it. Nicole remembers seeing something about 1-800-Flowers in his email. She turned the computer on and started looking for that mail. Sure enough she saw that Ramon ordered Vicki some flowers that came up to over $100 dollars. Nicole called him and asked him why he ordered flowers for Vicki. He said it was her birthday and the job asked him to order her flowers because he had an account with them. He said that everyone chipped in and gave him the money.

Nicole told Ramon that's ok because she would be at his job at 6pm. He told her not to come down there causing a scene. Ramon called Nicole later that day trying to sound really nice. He was asking her how she was doing and that he would come to the house. She told him that she was still going down to the job. She had so many questions about the things she found in the house. She remembered Ramon telling her that Vicki's boyfriend worked for the same company. He worked at a different branch. Nicole asked Ramon to give her his name and number so she could call him.

She wanted to see if he knew about their friendship. He said "Why do you want to mess up their relationship"? He told her that he was not giving her the number. She called that branch anyway. She asked the person that answered the phone to run down a list of the men's names that worked there. The guy started running down a few names. When he got to Jeremy, Nicole said "Yes that is him." She asked to speak to him. When Jeremy got to the phone, Nicole introduced herself. He said "Oh God, I need to speak to you." He asked could he please call her back from outside. Nicole gave him her telephone number.

He called back and she told him that she needed to ask him a few questions. He began to tell Nicole that he dated Vicki for four years and they broke up. He even left her for eight months and she never got over it. Even when they were not dating, they still acted like they were together. He said that someone at Ramon's branch told him that Ramon and Vicki were getting close. He did not want to believe it. He told Nicole how he had so much respect for Ramon. Ramon was married, saved, and he even asked Ramon to pray for him that they would get back together. He thought it was so strange that Nicole called him after he had been hearing things about them.

This young man was so hurt. Jeremy called Nicole about five times a day. He seemed like a really nice guy. He told Nicole that he was saved. He said that he went to Greater Deliverance Church. He told Nicole that he was working with the youth department also at his church. He said that he started going to church with Vicki but she eventually stopped going. He decided to stay in the church even though she was not going. He said that the job was taking her out for her birthday. He was not going because she told him that she wanted some time away from him. He asked her if she was seeing anyone and she said that she had a friend. At that time, he did not know where they were going.

Nicole spoke to Ramon on the phone. She never told him that she spoke to Jeremy. Nicole told Ramon that she needed to speak to him. She told him that if he comes to the house, she would not go down to his job. He said that he would be at her house around 8pm. Of course, he never came. Nicole was so angry. She called Jeremy and asked him if he found out where they were going. He said yes, and gave her the address. He told her to please keep him posted and tell him what happened. Nicole told him that she did not know if she was going. If she went she would call him.

Nicole sat around the house and she was so angry. She felt like she needed to know what was going on. Nicole called her friend Tabbie and asked her to take her to the restaurant. When they got there, she got out of the car and went inside the bar. Nicole walked to the back of the dark bar and what did she see. She saw Ramon sitting with his arm around Vicki and noticed he was not wearing his wedding band. Nicole was fuming. She did not know what to do.

There were two other guys from their job sitting at the table with them. Nicole tapped Ramon on his head and told him to come outside. He proceeded to follow her. She asked him "What was going on and why was his arm around her without his ring on?" He just kept saying "What?, what?". Nicole turned to Tabbie and told her what happened. Nicole walked back into the bar and said to Vicki, "Didn't I speak to you before. What's going on with you and my husband?" She looked up just as drunk as a skunk saying, "I don't want any problems. You have to ask him".

The funny thing is that Ramon and Vicki were the only ones that looked drunk. The whole time Nicole was yelling at her she kept her head down. Tabbie came into the bar and asked Nicole what was taking her so long. The next thing Nicole knew, Vicki must have hit Tabbie because she started tearing Vicki apart. Tabbie was throwing her around like she was a doll baby. Nicole was standing there in a state of shock. She did not know what was going on. Then Ramon came over and tried to help Vicki. Tabbie turned to him and started tearing him up also.

She had Ramon on the floor like he was a roach dying on his back. His arms and legs were kicking while he was on his back. Nicole started feeling really bad because she did not mean for this to happen. Nicole tried to pull Tabbie off of Ramon but she couldn't. Nicole's intentions were just to find out what was going on with Ramon. She did not know it was going to escalate into a big brawl.

A couple of people from the bar broke it up. Tabbie was no joke. Tabbie was Nicole's best friend since elementary school. She took the both of them on like she was the Heavy Weight Champion of the World. As they proceeded to walk out of the bar, Nicole looked back. Ramon walked over to Vicki and grabbed her by the waist. He was asking her if she was alright. He did not care what happened to his wife. Nicole's heart dropped when she saw that. After all she had done for him, he did that to her. She looked at him and walked out the bar.

Five minutes after they left the bar, Nicole called Jeremy to tell him what she had seen. She was going to tell him that the information was true. Before she could get it out, he started yelling "What did you do? What did you do?" Nicole told him that she did not do anything. He said "Well what did your friend do?" She said, "She did not do anything". Nicole told him that she was hanging up. She thought he wanted to find out if the information was true. Little did Ramon know, his so called friend Mike was the spy. Nicole knew something was fishy about him. When all the commotion was going on at the bar, he just sat there and did not budge. He was the one that gave Jeremy all the information. Mike was hanging around Ramon and Vicki and going back telling Jeremy everything.

The next day Vicki's family called Nicole's phone non-stop. They were calling all day. She constantly saw different numbers on her caller-ID. They were threatening to kill her. They said that they knew where she lived. They said she lived on Park Street. Mind you, she grew up on Park Street but that was not where she lived.   One of her cousins called and she said "Don't hang up." Her number showed up on Nicole's cellular phone. Nicole immediately called her older sister, Monique, who has a reputation of being a no nonsense person willing to fight for her family physically.   She called the person back. Nicole was sure that Monique's choice of words was not very pleasant. Then the girl explained that the only reason she called was to find out what happened. She began to tell Monique that Ramon told them that Nicole was crazy. He told them that they were in the process of a divorce and she was suicidal. He said that he left Nicole a long time ago and she tried to run him over with a car. He just told her family a bunch of lies about Nicole.

Jeremy told Nicole that he called Vicki's mother and told her that Ramon was married. She told Jeremy to give Vicki some space. She also told him that Ramon was in the process of his divorce. Lord only knows what else he told them. Ramon probably told her family that he was in law school etc. Jeremy had already told Nicole that Vicki's mother was not saved and was a heavy smoker. Nicole asked Jeremy if he thought that Vicki's mother would let Ramon stay with them. Jeremy told her "Yes". Nicole assumed that was where he was staying since he was not staying at his father's house.

Nicole could not understand how Ramon could be around Vicki's mother's smoking habit when he had asthma. Monique told Vicki's cousin that Ramon had been telling lies. She told her that Ramon said he was only going to be gone for a week. Her cousin began to tell Monique that it was good that Vicki got beat up. Her cousin said that Vicki knew better than to be messing with a married man. She told Monique to tell Nicole that she did not have to worry about another phone call. She was not lying because no one ever called her again.

About two weeks later, Nicole got home from church around 9pm. When she got home, her phone rang. You would not believe who was on the other line. The person said "Hello, may I speak to Nicole Williams". She said "speaking". He said this is Detective Johnson from the 67th precinct. He asked her if she beat up Vicki Lopez. Nicole told him that she did not beat anyone up. He said "Well she said you did". Nicole said "Well she lied". He asked her who was Tabbie? She told him a friend of hers.

He said well did Tabbie beat Vicki up? She told him that no one beat her up.

He told her that he needed the two of them to go down to the precinct to make a statement. Nicole asked him how he got her number. He said that Vicki gave it to him. She said, "Oh, so he gave her my number". He asked Nicole "Who are you talking about." Nicole answered, "Ramon." He asked, "Why would Ramon give Vicki your telephone number?" She said "because they are messing around." The cop said "Wait a minute. Who is Ramon to you?" Nicole said "My husband." He said "Oh now I got the story". He said Ramon is your husband and Vicki is messing around with a married man. Nicole said exactly. He told Nicole that she did not have anything to worry about. He still wanted them to come down and make a statement. He wanted them to come to the precinct Monday around 4:00 p.m.

After Nicole got off the phone with the detective, she could not stop shaking. She had never been involved with the law before and did not want to start now. She had a hard time trying to make a phone call. It seems like when she did make a call, no one was home. She decided to call her Uncle Butch. Thank God he was home. Her uncle retired from the police department. He used to investigate crooked cops. She told her uncle everything that happened. He wanted to hear Nicole's version and Tabbie's version before he called the detective. He was so upset with Ramon that he did not know what to do.

Nicole's uncle used to love Ramon. He took the detectives name and number and told Nicole that he would call her back. Uncle Butch called her back to tell her that he left a message for the detective to call him. Later on that night, Nicole's uncle called her back with some news. He said that he spoke to the detective and he told him that Nicole had a witness. The bartender at the club told the detective that she was standing there in a state of shock. Nicole did not know what the conversation was like but her uncle told her that she did not have to go to the precinct.

The detective told him that Nicole did not have anything to worry about. He was going to tell Vicki that they were going to counter sue her. Nicole's uncle told her that he would give the detective a week before he called him back. Nicole could not understand how the detective called her but failed to tell her that she had a witness. Nicole began to thank God for her uncle. If it were not for him and God, she would probably be in jail.

Uncle Butch called the detective a week later. Again, Nicole did not know what that conversation was about. Uncle Butch told her that the detectives said the case was officially dropped because Vicki never returned his calls. Uncle Butch told Nicole to go on with her life.

Nicole's brother Edward left numerous messages on Ramon's cell phone. Edward was trying to contact him to tell him, "If you are not going to be with my sister, get your clothes out of her house". He was not returning anyone's phone calls. Their Bishop even tried to contact Ramon but he would not respond. Edward decided that he was going to go to Ramon's job. He went down there with one of his friends. Edward told Nicole that when he got there and Ramon saw him, He got really scared. He told Edward to please wait one minute. Edward said he was in the back room for a long time. The next thing Edward noticed were the cops walking into the bank. Ramon had called the cops on her brother. The branch manager asked them to go into the back room. Edward explained to the cops that the only reason he went down there was because Ramon was not returning any phone calls. He said to the cops "Why would I come down here and do something with all these cameras on me?" He said after the cops finished listening, they told Ramon off.

He said "Look you have to be a man. I don't know how to tell you how to be one but you have to be one. This man just wanted to talk to you and you called the cops". Edward said the cops began to tell him what to tell Nicole to do. Ramon told Edward that he was getting off of work at 6pm and he would come outside and speak to him. Edward said that everyone came out the bank except Ramon. He said he waited a while then left.

Ramon called the house phone and left Nicole a long message. He said that Edward came down to his job with a bunch of guys in an unmarked car. He said that one of the guys kept pacing back and forth. He said that he felt threatened for his life. First of all it was only Nicole's brother and his close friend James. Secondly, the cops would have arrested them if they were in an unmarked car.

Ramon turned out to be such a liar. His true colors were really coming out.

Nicole's sister, Monique called him and gave him a piece of her mind. He had the nerve to tell Monique that he filed for legal separation. Nicole and her father went to the courthouse because she was going to file against him also. The clerk told them that he did not see anyone in the computer with that name. He said that they both would have to be there in agreement. Needless to say, Nicole never received any papers about a separation.

Nicole called Ramon on his cell and told him that he lied. She saw her brother before he left to go downtown. It was just Edward and one of his friends in the car. He told her that he called Edward and apologized for calling the cops. He said that he never brought harm to her. He said he was worried about her sister, Monique. He wanted to know if Monique was going to beat him up one time or beat him up a couple of times.

Nicole did not know that Ramon was a punk. He acted like he was tough. Nicole did not know what happened but Ramon was petrified of Monique. He used to tell Nicole how he used to fight all the time. He said that he was on the football team in high school and he would always get into fights. He said that he did not want to leave town because Nicole would not be able to get any money. Mind you, she has not seen a penny since he left. He wanted her to promise him that she would tell him what Monique was going to do. Nicole just let him sweat because she was not telling him a thing.

Nicole called Ramon and asked him when he was going to pick up his clothes. He had the nerve to tell her that he did not have a way of getting them. She told him to take a day off of work and rent a U-Haul and come and get his things. Carlton later told her that Ramon rented a car later that week. He could have easily gone and picked up his things. Nicole gave him until that Wednesday to get his things. He did not take her seriously because he just said, "yeah, yeah."

Ramon's father called Nicole and asked her to hold onto Ramon's clothes until Elder Williams came back from down south. She told him that she really did not want to but she would do it for him. When they came back from down south, she told them that they could pick his things up the next Friday. Friday ended up being a bad day for Nicole so she told them that they could pick up his things from her mother's house on Saturday. They started acting like they were the ones being inconvenienced. Ramon's father called Nicole and said that he did not want to be involved. He said that Ramon was going to handle his own business.

Elder Williams found out that his credit was still messed up when he went to rent the car. He had a problem with his credit. Ramon never took care of that credit card problem. Nicole and her sister, Monique, decided that if they were not going to pick up Ramon's clothes, they would take the clothes to them. They made arrangements with his father to take his clothes to his church.

Monique and Nicole dragged eight big garbage bags full of clothes, shoes, etc. to their cars. Everything could not fit in one car so they had to take Monique's jeep. He told us that he would be at Second Chance Church of God in Christ at 10:30am. Monique and Nicole got there at 10:00am. They thought the gate would have been open. They sat in front of the church until about 11:45 and the gate was still down. His father rolled up with other church members. Nicole could not understand why his father rode with someone else instead of driving his own van or car. He knew that they were bringing his clothes. Well anyway, Monique started dragging the bags out of the car and the jeep. Monique started throwing the clothes on the ground in front of the church. Mr. Williams and his sister Donna began to help drag the bags in the church. While all of this was happening, Nicole was videotaping everything. She had to have proof that she gave him his things. They then left the church.

Chapter 7

The Nightmare Is Almost Over

Nicole had not spoken to Ramon in a while but he decided to call on their wedding anniversary and leave a message. He said, "Hi Nicole, I know that today was supposed to be our wedding anniversary but I hope and pray that one day we can be friends."

One day Nicole was looking for a book on her bookshelf and she came across one of Ramon's journals. When she opened it, she began to read it. When she got to his last entry, she started to cry. He talked about how he wanted to die and was always afraid of death but today was a new day. He said how Nicole was always unhappy with him and that he had no reason to live because he disappointed everyone he loved. He said that all he ever wanted to do was to make Nicole happy. It was basically like a suicide note.

He needed help because he was clinically depressed. At the end of the entry, he stated that he hoped that this would not be his last entry but if it was, he hoped and prayed that one day Nicole could forgive him for everything. Nicole cried so much that she called Ramon on his cell phone. She almost forgot about everything he did.

She told him that all he has to do is repent and ask God to forgive him for everything he did. She told him that he should apologize to his family, Nicole's family and their church family. Nicole started to cry on the phone. Ramon told Nicole not to cry. He said please don't cry, he made her cry enough. He told Nicole that God was going to help her. She told Ramon that she was going to leave their church because she could not face the people. He said, "Don't leave the church; God is going to help you." He said that he did not want what he was doing to affect her. He said that he knew he was in the devil's hands.

Nicole told him that he had been in the church long enough to know how to get out of the devil's hands. He said he had been praying and reading his Bible. Nicole knew he was lying because he just said that he was in the devil's hands. If you are in the devil's hands, he is not going to give you a mind to pray and read your Bible.

Nicole could not understand why after all this man put her through, she was still trying to help him. She told him that when he was ready to talk, she would always be there for him. She told him that he could not keep everything inside. Ramon told her that he was not ready to talk about it. He said for her to know that when he does talk, she would be the first person he talks to. He really had her emotions running wild because she called him a couple of times trying to get him to talk. Nicole even told him that he was still on her insurance and he should schedule an appointment to see someone. There has to be a God because Nicole was still trying to help him.

Nicole found out that Ramon lost his job. She called his job one day and they told her that he was no longer with the company. When she spoke to Ramon, she asked him what happened to his job. He told her that he took a leave of absence. Nicole knew he was lying. Ramon would be the last person at the job if he could. His job did an investigation and found out that he was check kiting. Ramon was not too bright because he was check kiting from an account that was closed. He was putting the money into the bank where he worked.

Nicole was on the telephone with Carlton and he began to tell her that he was worried about his brother's behavior and was wondering if Ramon was on drugs. He didn't understand a lot of the things Ramon was doing and saying. Sometimes, Ramon even sounded delusional. Nicole said with a sad voice, "Carlton would call from time to time to check up on me and to say how sorry he was about what was going on with our marriage. Sometimes he would encourage me to keep hoping and praying that things would work out. He would remind me that God can do anything.

I had known Ramon's family for a very long time and although we weren't very close, I was really hurt, especially by his father's rejection. It felt like a slap in the face. So when Carlton would call to check on me, I felt good. It made me feel that everyone hadn't written me off.

I didn't have to wear my 'happily married' mask with him because he knew the truth." Carlton told Nicole how Ramon came home whenever he felt like it. "That's just not like him or the way we were raised." They would not see him for two or three days at a time. Carlton told Nicole how his father used to sit and wait for Ramon to come walking through the door. It was one mess after the other.

Nicole decided once again to call Ramon but he would not answer her phone calls. Nicole told Ramon's brother the next time he speaks to him to mention a divorce. Nicole told him to tell him to call her. Ramon called Nicole that same day. She was surprised. She guessed he spoke to Carlton. When Nicole answered the phone, he made her fall for his trick again. He sounded so sad that she could not bring up what she wanted him to call her for. He began to talk about how he did not know how long he was going to be here. He said that he was worried about himself. Yes, Nicole fell for it again.

One night when Nicole was sleeping in her bed, she was awakened by a scary dream. In her dream, she woke up kicking, screaming and punching. She opened her eyes in the dream and saw Ramon standing over her with a knife. When Nicole actually woke up, no one was there. She was so frightened that she could not go back to sleep. Her family told her that her dream could have meant that she did not know what next to expect from Ramon. Nicole did not know what that dream meant but she was scared. Carlton told Nicole a week later that he had a dream that Ramon came in their house with a knife while everyone was there. Nicole never told him about her dream. What was going on with Ramon and a knife?

The last straw was when Carlton told Nicole that Ramon said she was not a good wife. Nicole called Ramon on his cellular phone. He called her back, surprisingly. Before he could put on his sad voice, Nicole said, "What is going on with the legal separation?" He said, "I filed for it; did you get the papers?" She answered no; she had not received the papers. Nicole said forget those papers, let's talk about a divorce. Ramon was so shocked he did not know what to do. Ramon asked her to hold on a minute. Nicole said yes and he hung up on her. He called back maybe ten minutes later. The crazy thing was he called back just to ask her if he could call her back. He said something was wrong with his phone.

It was eight pm and he was on his way to get his cell phone fixed. It's common knowledge that the cell phone store closes at eight pm. Nicole told him that he was wasting time talking about the phone; he could have been talking about the divorce. She asked him why he did not call her from a payphone. He said because he did not have any change. She told Ramon to stop wasting her time. She told him "he better" call her back. He said that he would and he hung up. Of course, Nicole did not hear from Ramon for a couple of days.

Nicole left numerous messages on Ramon's cell phone talking about the divorce. He started leaving messages at the house when he knew she was not home. He left a message saying, "I got your messages. I know you want a divorce, I know you want out and I know you want to get rid of me. I will meet you on Friday or whenever it is convenient for you. I am going to grant your wish. I am sorry about the inconvenience." He said that he would call her later to make arrangements. He did not call her back so she called him the next day. Ramon thought Nicole already had the divorce papers. He said they could meet on Friday. She told him that she was going away for the weekend so Friday was not good for her. Nicole told him Monday was good and they agreed. He asked where they were going to meet. He decided for them to meet at Starbucks on 125th Street at 6:00 p.m.

Monday finally arrived and Nicole left a message on Ramon's cell phone. She asked him if he was still going to meet her at Starbucks. Instead of him calling her at her job or on her cell phone, Ramon left a message on her home phone. He left the message around 3:45 p.m. saying that he was not going to be able to meet her. He said that he was working a temporary job and they offered him some overtime. He knew he would have to help Nicole pay for half of the divorce. He wanted to make as much money as he could. He said that he would call her one day that week so they could reschedule.

Nicole's birthday was that Wednesday. He had the nerve to leave her a message saying, "Happy Birthday Nicole. I hope you have a fun day today. Just know that I am somewhere wishing you a happy birthday. I hope you enjoy your day sweetie." He left this long message about her birthday and did not mention anything about the divorce.

A week later, Nicole got home around 12:00 a.m. She called her mother to tell her that she made it home safely. Mrs. Watts told her that Ramon's family was trying to call her. Nicole never received a message from any of his family members. She said that they took him to the hospital because he was physically and mentally sick. Mrs. Watts suggested that they go out there. Mrs. Watts said that she would pick Nicole up in a little while. She took so long, Nicole ended up driving to her house to pick her up and her father.

When they got to the hospital, Mrs. Watts, Mr. Watts, Carlton, Jacob and Sandra stayed in the general waiting area. Nicole went into the Psychiatric Unit waiting area where his other sister, Donna, and his father were waiting. The first question Nicole was asked was "Is Ramon on your health insurance?" Nicole answered "No, I took him off a long time ago". Nicole assumed that was the only reason they wanted her to come out there. Elder Williams introduced Nicole to one of the doctors that had seen Ramon. He said that she would be able to speak to Ramon after the Psychiatrist got through with him. They said that Ramon had already spoken to three doctors. Nicole asked Mr. Williams and Donna a few questions and she went out to get some fresh air.

While Nicole was outside, the doctor that Elder Williams introduced her to was outside smoking a cigarette. He walked up to her and asked her what was wrong with Ramon? Nicole told him that she did not know. She was trying to find out for herself. He asked her if Ramon ever acted like that before and she told him not that she knew of. He said that Ramon keeps mentioning a divorce. He asked Nicole if they had any kids. She told him no. He asked where they live.

Nicole told him that they lived in the Bronx. He gave her a look like something was strange. Nicole told him that Ramon's father lives in Queens. His face had a sign of relief. The doctor thought Ramon did not know where he lived. He asked Nicole if Ramon worked. Nicole told him that she really did not know. He told her that he thinks Ramon is going to have to stay. Wow, Ramon finally was getting help. Nicole knew something mentally was wrong with all the lies and deceit.

Nicole walked back into the hospital and told Elder Williams and Donna that she would be back. She went back to the waiting area where Mr. and Mrs. Watts were. They sat out there and talked for a while. Sandra got up and went with her sister and father to the Psychiatric Unit where Ramon was. Approximately 10 minutes later, Nicole decided to go back to see if they finished speaking with him. As she was walking towards the Psychiatric waiting area, Elder Williams, Donna and Sandra were walking out. Nicole asked them what happened and where were they going? Donna said, "He left." Nicole said, "What do you mean he left?" Nicole could not understand how he was allowed to leave. Since the exit door was right near the waiting area. Donna said "He did not sign himself in so they let him go."

Elder Williams and Sandra were in agreement with Donna. Nicole ran back to where her mother and father were. She said, "Ma, they said Ramon left. Let's try to catch him." Nicole motioned for Carlton and Jacob to come outside. They did not know what was going on. Nicole noticed his family started walking in the opposite direction. Nicole called Carlton to come to her. He was asking her what was going on.

When he started walking towards her, Nicole guessed the family felt like they had to come that way. Mind you, their van was parked in the direction that Nicole was walking in. Nicole began to run around to the back of the hospital. Mr. Watts said that something was not right. God revealed to Nicole just that quick that no one had Ramon's bag. Nicole told her mother that nobody had Ramon's personal bag. When she first went into the Psychiatric Unit where Elder Williams and Donna were, she had his personal bag. Nicole told her mother that Donna was not that stupid to leave his bag at the hospital.

If Ramon left, they would not have given his personal property over to the hospital. Elder Williams began to say that there was nothing else they could do. He said that Ramon left. Mr. Watts ran down in the train station to see if he went down there. Nicole noticed that everyone in his family was walking nice and calm. Carlton and Jacob did not know what was going on. They all got in the van and

Elder Williams drove off. Nicole ran back to her mother and father. They did not find Ramon anywhere. Her mother told her to go back in to the hospital and ask the doctor what happened.

The guard remembered Nicole from before so he let her go back to the Psychiatric unit. Guess who she saw when she opened the door? She saw Ramon standing behind the glass. Nicole looked at him and waved. Ramon waved back. It took her a few seconds before she closed the door behind her. A sudden fear came over Nicole. (Maybe because she was in the Psychiatric ward all by herself) Once you came in through that door, you could not go back out that way.

Nicole felt a little better after she saw the guard. She closed the door and said to Ramon, "I thought you left." He said, "I did not leave. I am staying." Nicole told him that his family had said that he'd left. He responded again, "I did not leave. I am staying." Nicole said, "You're staying?" He said, "Yes." Then she noticed the duffel bag in the chair that Donna had before.

Ramon tried to walk away so Nicole could not see him. She saw him anyway. One of his nurses walked past. Nicole asked her what was going on with her husband. Nicole did not know what Ramon said in that room about her but the nurse talked to her like she was dirt. She started saying that Ramon did not want any information disclosed to her. He did not want anything to do with her. She said that Nicole needed to respect his wishes. He did not want her to bother him.

At that point, she could not even stick up for herself. Nicole could not believe she was talking to her that way. She had an angry expression on her face. Nicole stood there dumbfounded. Nicole relayed to the nurse that he was her husband and she wanted to know what was happening. She said, "Well, he is a grown man. He does not want me to tell you anything." Nicole told her, "Well, I'll just wait for him outside." Nicole did not know whether or not he was leaving or staying. He is the one that caused this problem and he did not want to see her.

She could have been wrong but she thought it should have been the other way around. At this point in her story, Nicole is mad! "They contacted me and I'm out there in the middle of the night with my parents only to have to deal with lies and insults!", she said angrily.

Nicole should have left him alone. Ramon must have really told them some lies. The crazy thing was that he was the one about to be admitted into the Psychiatric Unit and they believed everything he said. Ramon must have put up a big front for them. Even when Nicole saw him, he had his hands in his pockets. He was dressed in slacks and a dress shirt. He was still dressed like an important lawyer.

All she could remember thinking was where were her mother and father when she needed them. The exit door near that unit was in the back of the hospital. The time now was two o'clock in the morning and as she went outside, who did she see? She saw Ramon's family pull up in the van. They were so shocked to see her. As the Watts pulled off Sandra was saying something but Nicole could not understand her because she was in the back of the van. Nicole was asking Elder Williams what she was saying because she could not hear her.

Elder Williams did not look at Nicole one time. He even started to drive off slowly as she was talking. Nicole could not believe what was happening. She began to walk by herself in the back of the hospital at two-something in the morning. What kind of in-laws were they? How could they drive off while she was talking to them? It was dark outside and she was all alone running behind a van.

They did not care what happened to Nicole. They just drove off. Nicole ran into her dad. She told him what happened and he was very upset. They noticed the Williams van circling the block. They finally ran into Mrs. Watts. Mr. Watts and Nicole told her what had happened. They kept noticing the Williams van driving past the hospital. They were hoping Nicole and her family left. The Watts' found out later that Ramon was leaving from that entrance. Nicole understood that is why the Williams' was over there. Mr. and Mrs. Watts were so upset that they said they were leaving. Nicole could not understand why the Williams' called her family if they were going to lie. Oh, she remembers; they called for the insurance card. The Watts drove around to the front of the hospital to get to the highway. They noticed the Williams' sitting in the van in front of the hospital now. Nicole told her mother to stop the car. She wanted to give them a piece of her mind. Mr. Watts started saying to Nicole in a forceful voice, "Stay in the car."

Mrs. Watts got out instead and walked over to their car. Nicole is not sure what she said exactly. Nicole knew she told Elder Williams he should be ashamed for lying like that and reminded him he was an Elder. If Ramon did not want to see Nicole they never should have called her to the hospital. Nicole could imagine her mother said a lot because her mother is very outspoken, especially when it comes to someone lying. Mrs. Watts came back to the car and they drove off upset.

When they got back to the Watts' house, Nicole left them a message on the phone. She said, "Hello Williams' family. I would like to know the purpose of you all calling us if you were going to lie. As much dirt as Ramon did to me I still came out there to support him." She told them that either Ramon got them lying or he got it honestly. He probably got his lying from them. She also told them that she knew they were lying because Donna had his duffel bag. All of a sudden, they came out the hospital without the bag. She told Elder Williams that she was surprised at him. She never thought he would lie like that. Nicole wanted to stress that because he was an elder in the church. That is just a little bit of what she said and wanted to say because her mother told her to hang up the phone before she said the wrong thing.

The next day, Carlton called Nicole. He called to tell her that he felt really badly about last night and was confused. Nicole knew Carlton and Jacob did not know what was going on. Nicole was the one calling them to come outside. He began to tell her that it was not right. He was very upset with his family. He said that he told them that they did not have the right to waste Nicole's time. He said that she told them that she was still his wife and he knew Nicole left a message on the phone.

He said he ran to the machine and played the message. Donna, who started the lie, told him to erase the message before their father heard it. Carlton said no and played it over and over. He said Ramon heard it and just shook his head. He has some nerve after he caused this problem. Carlton said that they should have kept Ramon at the hospital because he really felt that his brother needed help and that his family was in denial about that fact. He said that Ramon had left again. No one knew when he left or where he went.

Nicole was so mad at that family that she decided to go to church with her mother that Sunday. She wanted them to see her after they lied to her and her family. As soon as they walked into the door, Elder Williams asked if he could speak to them downstairs. When they went downstairs, he began to apologize. He said that the doctor told him to tell them that. He said he did not know what to do at that point so he went along with it. Mrs. Watts started to tell him that no matter what the doctor said he is still an Elder. She told him that lying was not called for.

Nicole started feeling a little bad about the way she was talking to him but she did not let it show. He began to say that he did not know what else to do for Ramon. He gave Ramon two thousand dollars after he lost his job. Ramon told him that he needed it for stocks. Elder Williams said he had a bad dream one night. He felt that if he did not give that money to Ramon, something bad was going to happen to him. Mrs. Watts told him that if he constantly gave Ramon money, it would not help him but hurt him. He said that he knew but he didn't know what else to do. He began to cry, talking about how if he would have died; he would have gone to hell. He was crying so he could not finish his sentence.

All Nicole was thinking was that he was being phony because first of all, he did not bother calling her or her family on Saturday to apologize. If he would have died on Saturday, he would have been in trouble. Secondly, he did not know Nicole was coming to their church on Sunday because she is not a member there. One side of Nicole wanted to believe him but the other side of her was saying Ramon got it honestly. After he finished talking and Mrs. Watts said what she had to say, they gave him a hug and went upstairs.

When they went upstairs, Sandra and Donna were in the sanctuary. They would not look at Nicole to save their lives. She kept trying to get their attention but they would not look. Nicole walked past them twice and they didn't look her way. Mrs. Watts and Nicole decided to leave and go to her sister's church. As they were walking out the door, Jacob asked to speak to them outside. He began to tell them that he apologized for what happened. He said that he did not understand what was going on. Nicole told him the same thing she told Carlton.

She knew he did not know because she was the one that called them out there. He said that they were wrong for doing that. He also said that if Nicole did not care about Ramon, she would not have been out there. He said that the Williams don't like to tell him anything for some reason. He said that they need to get to the root of the problem. Nicole believes Ramon also had his family thinking she was the monster in the relationship. All along it was him. Nicole told him not to worry about it. Nicole knew he had nothing to do with what happened. He said that he would call Nicole and they left.

When Nicole got home that night, Carlton called her. He said, "Guess what?" She said what. He told her that Ramon almost wiped out Donna's bank account (the same sister that started the lie.) He got her information when he was staying with her for a little while. Nicole sent Sandra copies of some of the papers she found. She sent her the fake degree, resume, etc. Nicole figured it had to hit home before they would believe that something was wrong with Ramon. Carlton said that Donna just cried and cried talking about how Ramon needed to go to jail.

He said that Ramon also used her credit card to pay for his cell phone bill and a few other things. He told Nicole that Donna said, "I can't believe he did this to me and I lied for him." Well, God don't like ugly. He said that she was going to speak to a lawyer on Monday. She contacted the credit card company and they put a fraud alert on her account. She also had them contact his cell phone company and they turned his cell phone off. Now they do not have any means of contacting Ramon.

Nicole called Carlton on Monday to find out what happened. He said that they were not going to do anything about the fraud. He said that Elder Williams said that Ramon would not last in jail. Carlton got quiet for a few minutes and then said slowly, "Nicole, I think I'm going to have to stop being in contact with you. I see now that this situation is not really going to get any better and maybe, there is nothing I can do to help you or Ramon. At the end of the day, he's my brother. I care about you, Nicole, but I don't want him to resent me because I've been talking to you and now I kind of feel like I may be compromising my family.

I can't keep talking to you and not tell you the truth, but if I tell you what's being said and done...." "His voice drifted off," whispered Nicole, "and I knew that I had lost another person in my life and another connection to my husband". Nicole went on by saying, "The 'denial' that Carlton spoke about was Ramon's problem in the beginning. Being a late baby, he was spoiled and his parents let him get away with murder. But, you have to pay for your actions.

His family may not put him in jail but if he continues with these fraudulent acts, that is where he is going to end up."

Ramon's parents used to write him checks for school. He could not get along with Sandra. He acted like he hated her. Ramon told Nicole that he did not care what happened but Sandra was not going to be in their wedding. Nicole guessed it was because she was the only one that did not let him get his way. She told Nicole before that she told her mother to stop writing him checks until they found out if he was in school or not. She said that she asked her, "Why have we not seen a degree yet?"

On the other hand, he got along with Donna because all he had to tell her was a lie and she would write him a check. She had a good job. She was a nurse. She was not married nor did she have kids. So Nicole was sure he got a couple thousand out of her account. Carlton told Nicole that Ramon lied to his parents when he and Nicole first moved into their apartment. His parents gave him six hundred dollars because he told them that they were struggling with their rent. That was their mistake because they should have asked Nicole. As far as Nicole was concerned, they did not have a problem when it came to money.

Mrs. Watts asked Nicole to go to church with her on Saturday. Mrs. Watts' church was having a gathering session where everyone would come together. They would get together and talk about whatever they wanted to talk about. Mrs. Watts was the one teaching the class this day so she wanted Nicole to come. Mrs. Watts told Nicole that Ramon's sisters never come but they were both there that day. Nicole recalls one lady saying how she and her husband got back together. Another lady was talking about how she and her mother did not get along. Mrs. Watts told everyone that they had to say something. Everyone that was there said something. Nicole was the last one to speak. Mrs. Watts handed her the microphone.

Nicole began to share her personal business with the church. Any other time, she would not have said anything. Since Donna and Sandra were there, she felt like she wanted to put it out in the open. They were forever trying to cover up the wrong in their family so she let it out. She still did not feel comfortable telling someone that she never had sex with her husband. Ramon always talked about how his family always tried to act like the perfect family.

Nicole started off by saying, "Ernestine, I am happy that you and your husband are back together. I guess while your husband was coming home, mine was walking out the door." Nicole went on from there. It is funny how Sandra and Donna never apologized to her until she told her business. Donna came over to her crying telling her that she was sorry and she loves her. Sandra never apologized but she said that she loves Nicole and is there for her.

Nicole never took them at their word. In all the years that Ramon and Nicole were together, they never called them. She never heard from his side of the family after that. Nicole would call Carlton from time to time to see how he was doing. She had nothing else to do with the rest of the family. They never called to check up on her so she never called them. (Hey, Nicole wasn't their blood so she guessed she never really expected them to.)

Nicole was talking to her friend Tabbie. She does not know how they got on the subject of Nicole's book collection. She mentioned a famous author named Joe Lindenburg. He was an author that they said was gay. Ramon had his whole collection. Nicole never read those books so she did not know what they were about. Nicole decided to read one of the books and a lot of things that went on in one of the books seemed to match what Ramon lied about.

There was also something that Ramon carried that one of the book's characters carried. Nicole never bought Vaseline so she could not understand why Ramon always had to have Vaseline in his bag. Nicole never, ever saw him put it on his face or lips. Nicole called Carlton and asked him if he suspected that Ramon was gay. He said that he did not appear to be that way. He said that he kept talking about one of their church members named John. Now John was a person who went to their church. Ramon could not stand him because he was gay. He acted like he could not stand gay people.

Now Nicole was hearing the person he could not stand, he was telling his brother that was his friend. He said he talked about him a lot. He used to hate for Carlton to hang around him. He always said that he needs to act like a man. Nicole remembers one time Carlton went with them to church. Ramon was very upset because Carlton did not respond to men the way he wanted him to. He wanted him to be rough and tough. Nicole wondered if Ramon was gay all along.

No one heard from Ramon in a long time. According to Carlton, they had not heard from Ramon either. Ramon was hiding out. Nicole did not know how much longer he thought he could run. Nicole believed he planned to hide for the rest of his life. She believed that Ramon had a new identity. She believed he changed his name. Nicole called Elder Williams and asked him to file a missing person report with the precinct. Elder Williams told Nicole that there was too much red tape involved. She asked him what he meant by too much red tape. He began to ramble on about something but never answered her question. Nicole told Elder Williams to forget it; she was going to file for it since he did not want to do it. Nicole thought that his father had to file for it since one of the last places Ramon stayed was his father's home.

Nicole and her mother went to the precinct to file a missing person report. The civilian worker asked what took her so long to file. Nicole explained that she thought his father was supposed to file. He then asked her how old Ramon was. When Nicole answered, the worker explained that Ramon was old enough to leave on his own accord. Mrs. Watts then said, "So what is the purpose of a missing person report?" He said that it was usually used for people with a mental disability, a child or an elderly person.

Nicole showed him Ramon's journal where he was talking about dying. He read a few sentences from the journal and started filling out the report. After the worker finished filling out the report, Nicole and Mrs. Watts left. When Nicole got home, she had a message on her telephone from the civilian worker. He told her that it was very important that she call the precinct. He said that because of the journal, they were putting Ramon into a different sector. Nicole called the worker back and he told her that he tried to catch her before she left. He said that he wanted her to come back to the precinct. She told him she could not go but they could send someone over to her house. Nicole called one of her friends, Bobby, who is a police officer to get some advice. The cops never came or called. Bobby called the precinct and spoke to someone who told them they were still coming to the house.

The cops rang her bell at twelve am. She was home by herself and very nervous. She opened the door to three big Caucasian cops. They came inside the house and asked Nicole a few questions. They told her that they wanted her to call Elder Williams. The officer wanted to speak to him. She got Elder Williams on the telephone. One of the officers was in the kitchen talking to him while she was in the living room with the other two officers.

They told Nicole that they had to take the book as evidence. They said because if he is found dead, that is proof that she did not kill him. They continued to ask Nicole questions. When the officer got off the phone with Elder Williams, Nicole asked the cop what he said. The officer told Nicole he said that Nicole and Ramon were separated. He also told them Ramon stayed with him for a week and he thought

Ramon went back home. There he goes once again telling a lie. Nicole spoke to Elder Williams the day before she made the report. He kept saying that he did not hear from Ramon either.

He knew for a fact that Ramon was not at Nicole's house. Ramon just left and tried to disappear. Elder Williams also contradicted himself. If they were separated, why would he think Ramon came back to her house? Nicole told the cops that she believed Elder Williams knew something because he was lying. Maybe Elder Williams did not know what to do or say once again.

 Nicole told them that it was impossible to believe that someone is going to disappear and you are not going to try and find him. What kind of father is that? Nicole was glad that he was not her father. His son disappeared for four months and instead of trying to find him, he threw his hands up. Well that sounded like he knew something. When Nicole said that, all three cops shook their heads at the same time and said, "You're right." The officers left and told Nicole that she would be hearing from a detective in a few days.

Monique called Vicki and told her that Nicole was trying to get in touch with Ramon because she wanted a divorce. Vicki told her that they were in a relationship. Vicki told her that Ramon told her that Nicole filed for the divorce. Of course, Ramon was starting his new relationship lying. What goes around comes around. She knew he was a married man. Nicole was not sure what their conversation was about. The only thing Nicole knew was that Ramon called her house that same night. Nicole was not home so he left a message. Ramon tried to sound professional. He was using his lawyer voice. He said, "Hello Nicole, I was calling to get Monique's telephone number. I am going to be cooperative with the divorce proceedings. I promise to call you tomorrow to make arrangements to meet so we can get the divorce expedited. Thank you." When Nicole heard the message she just wanted to throw up.

Nicole had a feeling that Vicki was sitting right there when he called. He had the nerve to sound like everything was okay and he was so important. Ramon called the next day which was Saturday. Nicole finally spoke to him. Nicole asked Ramon why he was hiding out. He just said, "I just want to be cooperative." He did not want to answer any questions.

He just wanted her to know that he was going to cooperate. Nicole then told him, "Well, I wanted a divorce a long time ago and you disappeared." He said, "Yes, well I'm back now." Nicole asked Ramon where they were going to meet. He told her downtown on Wilson Street. She asked him why all the way down there. He said because he was down there. She asked him why she was supposed to make it easy for him. Nicole told him they were going to meet at 197th Street and to bring his half of the money. he proceeded to ask her for Monique's phone number. She hesitated but gave it to him anyway. She wondered...why does he want to call my sister? She put her thought to the side and reminded him of the meeting plans.

Chapter 8

Please Release Me. Let Me Go!

Ramon called Nicole on Monday around three thirty to cancel the meeting. Nicole was not going to pick up the phone at first. She decided to pick it up and he began to tell her that he could not meet her because he had to work. That was the same excuse he gave her months ago. He asked her could they meet that following week. She told him no we can meet Thursday or Friday. Then his excuse about working changed to his legal representation was not going to be available that week. Nicole told him that she needed to know what day he was talking about so her lawyer would be available. He said that he would call her on Friday to let her know. She reminded Ramon about bringing his money. She also asked him if he was going to pay for legal fees.

He said that they agreed to split the bill. Nicole told him that she never agreed to anything. He said they can discuss that when they meet. Ramon then said, "Thank you so much Nicole." She did not know what he was thanking her for but she just said goodbye and hung up. Nicole believed that Vicki was not there for that phone call.

Carlton called Nicole and told her that Ramon had appendicitis and had to have surgery. He was in the hospital for six days. He was in there for Thanksgiving. He found out because a bill came to the house for forty four thousand dollars. Representatives from Brooksdale Jewish Hospital came to Elder Williams' house to collect the money. They explained Ramon had appendicitis and had to have immediate surgery. Ramon gave them his correct name, correct address, incorrect telephone and incorrect social security number. Elder Williams told them that he did not see him in months and no one called to tell him Ramon was sick. The representative from Brooksdale Hospital left after that.

It had been eight months and no one still heard from Ramon. Although it was less frequent than before, Carlton kept in touch with Nicole, most of the time just to ask how she was doing. He was the only family member that showed concern about her well-being. Carlton called Nicole and told her that he went by Vicki's job. He explained, "I know I said I was going to stop calling you and stay out of my brother's life but I hate that you have been hurt and I don't want to see anyone else hurt because of my brother's problems."

Carlton had not gone to Vicki's job alone; he took his friend with him. He had his friend to ask for Vicki because he thought she would be a little uneasy about speaking to him. Carlton's friend walked over to the counter and said, "I'm here to see Vicki Roman." The person asked who he was. He told them that he and Vicki went to school together. When Vicki came out the back room, he yelled, "Hi Vicki." She looked at him as to say, "Where do I know you from?"

That is when Carlton walked over and introduced himself as Ramon's brother. She immediately told Carlton that he was not Ramon's brother but was his cousin. Carlton began to tell her that Ramon had been lying to her about his real name. She said, "I love Randy. He is very intelligent. He has so many degrees. He is very educated and I really like that". Carlton shouted, "Ramon, you are so stupid because his name is not Randy." She replied, Yes it is." Carlton then showed her Ramon's birth certificate and some other papers with his name on it. She just kept repeating how much she loved him. She told Carlton that Ramon said the divorce went through. She also said that Ramon told her he was much younger than he was.

Everything Carlton said seemed to be going in one ear and out the other. Ramon was a very good liar! Nicole never met anyone else who could look you in the face and tell a bold face lie. Ramon was very convincing, that is why he fooled so many people. He should have gotten a standing ovation for fooling the very elect. Carlton asked Vicki why she did not tell his family that he was in the hospital. She said that Ramon called his mother and told her. Nicole wondered how he did that when she had already passed away. She also said that Ramon did not want anything to do with the rest of the family.

Carlton got mad and said well if he doesn't want anything to do with them, tell him to stop sending his mail to our address. Vicki let the cat out of the bag when she told him that Ramon worked at China Federal Bank. Carlton asked her where and she said she was not going to repeat it. Little did she know, she gave Carlton enough information to find China Federal. (Can you believe he got another job at a bank?) Carlton called the main branch and found out what location Ramon was working.

Carlton called the branch and the person that picked up the phone said that he was off for the day. She said that he would be back on Tuesday. Carlton went down to his job on Tuesday. When he got there he asked for Ramon Williams. The person went in the back room. She came out and said, "Oh, I am sorry. I misunderstood who you asked for. No one by that name works here." Carlton told her thank you and left.

The next day, Carlton called Ramon on the three-way at the bank. He even had this new branch lying for him. He told Nicole not to say anything. He just wanted her to hear the conversation. Carlton said, "Hello Ramon." Ramon took a long pause. Nicole guessed he was wondering how they found out where he was. Carlton began to call him an adulterer and a few other things. All Ramon could say was

"Whatever". Carlton told him that he was going to Hell. Ramon asked him, "Where do you think you're going?" He said "Look at your lifestyle." Then he said words to Carlton that are hard to forgive and impossible to forget, "GO FIND YOUR REAL MOTHER." He told Carlton that he did not have any ties with him and for him to go and call his mother. Ramon was really trying to be hurtful. Although Carlton was adopted as an infant, he was more of a son to Elder and Mrs. Williams than Ramon ever was. Ramon then said, "I don't speak to gays." Then he hung up the phone.

Carlton and Nicole were not going to give up until they saw Ramon. They found out where Vicki's mother worked. Nicole called Monique and told her about it. Monique made arrangements for all of them to go and pay a surprise visit to Vicki's mother. Ms. Roman was a cleaning lady at Bethany Hospital. When they got to the hospital, they asked the cop where the housekeeping department was. He sent Monique and Nicole down a long hallway and told them to use the wall phone. They called but no one answered. They then went upstairs to the housekeeping office. The manager said that Ms. Roman was out to lunch.

One of the gentlemen that were standing there took them down to the telecommunications department. They paged Ms. Roman to come to the front desk. They waited about ten minutes and she never came up. They paged her again. She came upstairs about five minutes later. When she saw them, she did not know who they were. Monique walked up to her and said, "Hello, Ms. Roman. My name is Monique and this is Ramon's wife. We are not here for any trouble. We would like to speak to you." Ms. Roman said, "Sure let's go outside because I want to smoke a cigarette." When they went outside, they began to tell her everything. They also showed her proof. She kept saying, "Oh, my God, I knew something was wrong with him. I told my mother something was wrong."

Ms. Roman told us that when she was home alone with Ramon, he would listen to her conversations when the phone rang. She said she would notice the television on loud but then when she got on the phone, she could barely hear it. She said that her daughter begged her to let him stay because he had nowhere else to go. She told them that Ramon said he did not have any family. Ramon told them that his father put him out. He told her that Nicole was manic depressive and the divorce had already gone through.

He told her that he graduated from New York College. (What happened to Shoreway University?) He basically told them a bunch of lies. She also said that her daughter was hard-headed. She had just gotten over a bad relationship and she should wait before jumping into another relationship. Vicki would not listen to her. Ms. Roman agreed to have them surprise Ramon at her house on Sunday after church.

Nicole called Ms. Roman on Thursday night just to make sure that plans did not change. She told them that nothing had changed and that she did not tell him anything. She called Nicole back on Friday and told her that she did not want everyone to come to the house, only Nicole and Elder Williams. Nicole told her that Ramon, the con artist deceived so many people and they were all going to come. Nicole told her that they did not have to come into her house. They would talk to him in the hallway. They just wanted to make sure he was there. Ms. Roman changed her mind and said its okay, everyone can come.

On Sunday, Nicole met up with Mr. and Mrs. Watts, Monique, Carlton and Johnny. Johnny is a friend who went to church with them years ago. Elder Williams and his sisters did not want to come. Nicole spoke to Ramon's sister Sandra on the telephone after they met with Ms. Roman. She felt that she just wanted to pray for Ramon. She did not feel it was her place to go to the house. She said that Ramon felt betrayed when they called Nicole to the hospital. He sure ran a good guilt trip on them. It was sad to say, excluding Carlton, he was taking that family for a ride.

Elder Williams must love getting robbed of his life's earnings. He did not go to the apartment. When Nicole and her family arrived at the apartment, no one was home. Monique called Ms. Roman on her cell phone. She said, "No one is home. You guys took too long." They had a feeling she said something to Ramon. Monique got upset and said, "Ms. Roman, God bless you, don't say you were not warned," and she hung up. Ms. Roman called them back two minutes later and told them that they were on their way back home. When they got off the elevator,

Nicole's group knew they had been at someone else's apartment because no one had their coat on. Mind you, it was cold outside. They all walked into the apartment. Ms. Roman told them to have a seat. Mrs. Watts started the conversation. She asked Ramon, "Why?" Ramon said, "Why what?" She said, "Why did you have to lie?" She told him that he was supposed to be saved and his whole life was full of lies. By this time, Mrs. Watts knew about the sexual dysfunction.

Ramon looked like the devil. He kept looking evil at Carlton and Nicole. He had put on a lot of weight. He was sitting there like an evil stuffed pig. Everything Nicole brought up he lied about. He said that he did not finish college but he was three credits away. He said that he did not use his father's social security number. Mind you, Elder Williams got his credit report and found that he just opened three new accounts with his father's social security number. On one of the cards, he spent ten thousand dollars, on the other card he spent two thousand and they were not sure what was on the third card. Everything that Ms. Roman told Monique and Nicole, he denied. He just continued to lie and lie. He claimed that someone kept calling his cell phone threatening him. Nicole asked him if it was a ghost. He said, "I felt afraid for my life. That is why I did not call for the divorce."

Nicole was wondering what he was afraid of. What were they going to gain by hurting Ramon? Absolutely nothing! That was his crazy mind that had him going. Remember, he was the one in the psych ward. He assumed it was

Monique calling him on the phone. Maybe that was some of the lies he also told his family. That is why they felt they had to hide everything. Nicole wanted to tell Ramon's family he was not worth her or her family going to jail. When they finished with Ramon they left. Mrs. Watts went back into the apartment with Johnny. We stayed in the hallway. When Mrs. Watts came out, her face was red and flushed. She said that she got very angry with him. She began witnessing to him and telling him that he needed to go back to church. She also asked him if his sexual disability was true. He said yes and he made a choice to live sex free. Lie #1,999 because there was no way in the world Vicki was going to be with someone who can't perform. (Then again, Nicole did it so why wouldn't Vicki.)

Ramon knew how to wine and dine you and tell you that he wanted to wait until marriage before having sex. Unless, Vicki saw some of those dollars he stole. He mastered spoiling a person with gifts, flowers and money. A con artist knows how to reel you in completely and then later you will see the bomb explode. Maybe he was giving Ms. Roman money also. Maybe she felt her daughter struck it rich this time. Ramon already had them thinking he had all these college degrees.

Common sense would say, if he has all those degrees, why would he be working at a bank as a customer service representative and be doubled up in a two bedroom apartment in the projects with Vicki and her family. Before they left Vicki said, "The lawyer can call the house."

Nicole guessed she told her right there that she was not giving up her man for no one. Ramon never apologized for anything. He did not seem remorseful at all. Mrs. Watts came out and they left.

Carlton called Nicole and told her that Ramon pawned his wedding ring. He told her which shop the ring was sold. Nicole and Monique went to the pawn shop and purchased back the ring she bought for thousands for only $100. This was the actual the last time that Carlton reached out to Nicole. Maybe helping her get her ring back was his way of helping her get closure on this very bad experience.

Nicole believed Ramon could never keep up with his lies. Once you tell one lie, you have to keep telling lies. His life was full of lies. The sad part is that he dragged other people into it. Nicole believes Vicki was a cover up. Ramon probably used her to cash those checks at the bank since she was a teller. Nicole feels like she could have been a cover up also. Maybe Ramon married her so no one would know he was possibly gay. Nicole believes he wanted her to find that journal. It was amazing how quick everything came out. You never realize things until it's too late.

Thinking back, Nicole remembers that he only read from the two same law books all the time. Even when he graduated and went to another school, he STILL acted like he was studying from the SAME two law books. She shook her head in shame, "No one picked up on anything." Ramon fooled a lot of people. Ramon was doing church functions but did not know God. He was in the church but the church was not in him. Nicole could not understand how he was not convicted for what he was doing. He went to the church every Sunday giving God praise.

There has to be a God somewhere. When Nicole thinks of what Ramon could have done to her, she just cries. One blessing was that they did not have any kids. Not consummating the marriage was a blessing in disguise. If he was having sexual relations outside of the marriage, he could've passed terminal diseases to her. Even when Ramon left, she was able to pay all her bills. The good thing about it was that everything was in her name. She thanked God because she could have had to give up her apartment. The car dealership could have repossessed her car. The greatest victory is that she is still in her right mind. She is able to function and live life. She did not end up in a mental institution.

Nicole is not pretending that she does not get sad sometimes. She gets down but then she picks herself back up. She was with this man for many years. That shows that it does not matter how long you are with a person. You may never know who that person really is. She even thinks about how God allowed her to use his health insurance. If she used her own insurance, she probably would have had a hysterectomy. He could have wiped out her bank account. He could have stolen everything she had in the house. Nicole has a beautiful home, nice car, a good job, good credit and peace of mind. Nicole is not going to say that she does not think about what Ramon did to her.

The only good thing is that it could have been much worse. It could have also lasted for years and years. Nicole's story reminded her of a case that was in the newspaper. The only thing was that the guy pretended to be a doctor and he killed his wife and child once she caught on to him. Thank God for Monique because Ramon was obviously too scared to go that route. They may never know why Ramon did what he did. He just might take it to his grave. Maybe in his messed up mind, he believes he has done no wrong.

Eventually, due to New York State spousal abandonment laws, her divorce was finalized. Nicole was sad and relieved on the day she received her paperwork. Sad about the failed marriage and the death of the dream she had held onto that she and Ramon would be the ideal, God-fearing couple. With the death of that dream, she knew she would never be that same starry-eyed, naïve, timid girl that she was on her wedding day.

Even though she was sad, she was relieved, that she now was officially free of a situation that had been a weight on her mind and spirit. This was a weight that the enemy had tried to establish as a stronghold in her life. A stronghold that would keep her bound forever. But God!! Looking back, Nicole could see how the hand of a good God had kept her, provided for her and been her Comfort and Company! Even before she could reveal this painful period of her life to others, before she decided to cry out and loose the bands of deception --- God had been there with her. He had made it possible for her to emerge a stronger, wiser, better woman. She is living proof that you don't have to look like what you have been through. To God Be the Glory!

Chapter 9

Hold On To Your Faith

There are times we don't understand why there are trials in our lives. We walk around with our heads hung low. Little do we know that these trials are there to make us strong. While going through these times, we should stay prayerful and read the Word of God so we can overcome what life throws at us. God will work it out as long as you keep your faith in him. *"For we walk by faith, not by sight."* 2 *Corinthians 5:7*

Believe God even if you do not see your way out. *"Now faith is the substance of things hoped for and the evidence of things not seen."* *Hebrews 11:1* God did it for me so I know he can do it for you. God loves each and every one of you reading this book. He will not put more on you than you can bear.

I decided to tell my story to encourage, strengthen and to free everyone who is going through the same things I've come through and let them know that they are not alone. You too can be a victor and not a victim if your faith is in Christ. I realize now that the main prison the enemy tried to keep me in was silence. I pray you decide to confide in someone, whether it be a pastor, a family member or a close friend, if you find yourself in a painful situation. I regret not speaking to someone about what was happening in my life. I chose to deal with it all alone.

I went to great lengths to isolate myself from people who had been my friend for many years. I was ashamed. And that shame made me want to hide. You may never get an apology or an explanation for the horrid things that people do to you, but just release yourself and let it go! It does not help you to keep it locked inside. Tell someone about it. Free yourself. Now I am on the journey of healing and forgiveness - forgiveness of myself and the person who wounded me so deeply. That's real freedom. To know that nothing can separate me from God's love – not even the deepest pain --- that's real freedom! And guess what? Sabrina and I are still friends but I am now officially speaking up for MYSELF! This little song is part of my testimony:

> God will take care of you,
> God will take care of you,
> Satan is a liar and a deceiver too,
> But God will take care of you.

CPSIA information can be obtained
at www.ICGtesting.com
Printed in the USA
BVHW081956090123
655921BV00004B/58